PURPLES' EDITION

OF THE REVISED

STATUTES OF ILLINOIS.

1856.

THIS REVISED EDITION OF THE STATUTES OF ILLINOIS includes all the Laws complete to 1856—all those prior to and since the revision of 1845. At the end of each Law the decisions of the Supreme Court are given, making it an indispensable book to the Lawyer and Student — saving them time and expense.

PUBLISHED BY

KEEN & LEE.

AT THE

CHICAGO LAW BOOK STORE.

NO. 148 LAKE STREET,

CHICAGO, ILLINOIS.

W. Richardson,

Galveston,

Texas.

State Capitol, Iowa City.

IOWA AS IT IS

IN 1856;

A GAZETTEER FOR CITIZENS,

AND A

Hand-book for Immigrants,

EMBRACING A FULL DESCRIPTION OF

THE STATE OF IOWA:

HER AGRICULTURAL, MINERALOGICAL, AND GEOLOGICAL CHARACTER; HER WATER COURSES, TIMBER LANDS, SOIL AND CLIMATE; THE VARIOUS RAILROAD LINES BEING BUILT AND THOSE PROJECTED, WITH THE DISTANCES ON EACH; THE NUMBER AND CONDITION OF CHURCHES AND SCHOOLS IN EACH COUNTY; POPULATION AND BUSINESS STATISTICS OF THE MOST IMPORTANT CITIES AND TOWNS.

INFORMATION FOR THE IMMIGRANT

RESPECTING THE

SELECTION, ENTRY, AND CULTIVATION OF PRAIRE SOIL, A LIST OF POST-OFFICES IN THE STATE, ETC. ETC.

WITH NUMEROUS ILLUSTRATIONS.

BY NATHAN H. PARKER,
CLINTON, IOWA.

CHICAGO, ILL.:
KEEN & LEE,
1856.

STEREOTYPED BY J. FAGAN, PHILADELPHIA.

PRINTED BY SMITH & PETERS.
Franklin Buildings, Sixth Street, below Arch,
Philadelphia.

TO

THE YOUNG MEN OF IOWA,

INTO WHOSE HANDS WILL, ERE LONG, BE ENTRUSTED THE DESTINY OF OUR YOUNG STATE, AND BY WHOM HER FREE SOIL, HER BOUNDLESS RESOURCES, AND HER REPUBLICAN INSTITUTIONS, ARE SOON TO BE DEVELOPED, CONTROLLED, IMPROVED, AND PERPETUATED,

THIS BOOK IS RESPECTFULLY

Dedicated.

THAT THEY PROVE WORTHY OF THE SACRED TRUST, NEVER SWERVING FROM THE PATH OF DUTY, AND THAT THEY EXERT THEIR PREROGATIVES AS FREEMEN, TO ADVANCE INTO AN EVER-EXPANDING PROSPERITY THE NOBLE STATE WHOSE HELM THEY HOLD, IS THE DESIRE AND HOPE OF

THE AUTHOR.

CONTENTS.

CHAPTER XIV.

CHAPTER XV.

CHAPTER XVI.

CHAPTER XVII.

CHAPTER XVIII.

CHAPTER XIX.

CHAPTER XX.

CHAPTER XXI.

CHAPTER XXII.

CHAPTER XXIII.

CHAPTER XXIV.

CHAPTER XXV.

CHAPTER XXVI.

CHAPTER XXVII.

CHAPTER XXVIII.

CHAPTER XXIX.

CHAPTER XXX.

PREFACE.

After a careful arrangement of information compiled by piecemeal, during a twelvemonth passed in the editorial chair, and during that period subjected to constant revision and pruning—after the receipt from the several counties in our State, of the latest statistical intelligence relating to each—and as the general result of two year's attentive study—it is that the Author has been enabled to prepare his work for the public eye. He is aware that an occasional error may have crept into it, or that here and there a piece of information may have been omitted, but he trusts and believes that the pains he has taken to avoid these have not been in vain, and that if any are found, they will be as few as possible, and in no case, of great importance.

It is the design and aim of the Author in presenting his book to the public, to supply a want that has long been felt, and which is being daily expressed, as well by the present resident in Iowa, as by the countless throng still pouring westward, and the thousands in the crowded East, whose thoughts and aspirations turn towards us.

Iowa holds out to the emigrant inducements such as no other State in our Union can boast, nor is any other at this day being so largely flooded by the onward tide of immigration. Her resources are inexhaustible, her advantages are beyond the scope of calculation, and her claims upon the attention of every class and sex of the energetic, the industrious and the ambitious, are as peremptory as they are vast. Yet is there a deplorable scarcity of such published information as shall set forth these latent sources of wealth.

The eastern traveller and emigrant; the western resident — whether he be but a new-comer, or whether he has risen to fortune in our midst — and the State itself, require such an exposition as the Author has attempted in the following pages. If he has succeeded in representing, according to its deserts, "Iowa, as it is in 1856" — if his task shall tend to throw a light over the immigrant's path, or to erect a guide-board upon his way—if his work will serve to eradicate or lessen whatever of misconception or of prejudice may have existed in the minds of strangers—if, as the fruit of his labors, he shall be able to induce others to join the mighty host that even now is swarming to Iowa's fertile fields — if, in fine, he has been able to place Iowa before the world, in its true light, and to assign to it that lofty rank among the States which it must attain and forever hold—he will feel that he has not fallen short of the elevated goal of his ambition, and, in the consciousness of a duty fulfilled will reap a golden reward.

And here the Author feels called upon to express the gratitude he feels towards those to whom he has applied for information. With scarcely an exception, he has met with prompt and kindly answers, and an earnest co-operation. And while thus returning his thanks, he would ask of those who have aided him heretofore, as well as of any who may bestow their attention upon his book, to further assist him, and whenever they may detect aught that is erratic, or discover any omission, to inform him in the matter, that he may be able, in future editions to rectify the one and fill up the other.

IOWA, *May*, 1855.

INTRODUCTION.

Still fresh in the memories of a few of her citizens, is the time when Iowa was one vast wilderness. Her land untilled, her groves unpeopled, and her mighty rivers flowing unimpeded — unadmired, by art or eye of man, she donned her verdant robes, and decked her fields with flowers on each returning spring, as if to woo the distant husbandman, and when chill autumn came, she shrank again into the sere and withered, waiting, patient still, and still with hope. She heard the Indian hunter's shot resound amid her solitude; she held the imprint of his step upon the yielding surface of her soil; she watched him crawl to his wigwam home, and lay him down to slothful rest, to dream of the ravage or the hunt. She saw him wake from sleep, and gird about his loins the savage tomahawk and scalping knife, while piercing war-whoops rang from dell to dell, and whistling balls and rolling thunders shook the air above, and bathed the blazing fields in gore. She heard the red man's cry of death — the white man's shout of victory. And then her streams and fields — her hills and waving woodlands—joined in one vast choral hymn, when banners were furled, and arms were lain to rest, and Peace snatched the sceptre from the wearied God of War.

Then, soon, throughout the land, a lamentation rose. The red man stretched his form upon the earth, and bathed the sod with tears. He bade a long farewell to hunting-ground and river-bank — to bluff and valley, where transcendent beauty held her court, or uttered a parting wail beside the graves of his fathers—the mounds of his nation's slumbering chiefs. Here, from year to year, had successive generations learned to kneel — here had their voices risen annually, in strains of mourning and of homage, for the loved or the illustrious dead—here had been their refuge in times of sorrow or of trouble—and here had they found a retreat, sequestered from the world, and hedged round with a sacred—an unprofaned reverence. But although he lingered still—although to leave these solemn scenes occasioned him most poignant grief—called forth the wildest throes of anguish—yet, inexorable fate impelled the red man onward. Civilization required his departure;—the destiny of his outcast race bade him fly from before the coming white man's face, and take another step towards that extinction which yawns before the savage tribe. He raised his voice, once more, in cries of anguish, then joined the mighty Ishmaelitish host, and, taking up the line of march, he pressed his farewell foot-print on his native soil, and left behind him on the spreading plains, the last Indian trail of Iowa.

E'en yet the heavy tramp of the banished nation sounds along the western horizon—e'en yet that horizon is blackened by the forms of the retreating multitude—when lo! upon the east a long white line comes gleaming up, seemingly rising out of the distant ground. One by one, like sails at sea, the white-tented wagons of the immigrant well up into sight, and soon we shall see their occupants encamped near yonder grove, their tents gleaming in the moonlight, and the smoke of their camp-fires spreading like a protecting shelter, above their deep, untroubled slumbers. These hardy men, with their aged parents and adolescent families, moving onward in the wake of the expatriated Indian, are the pioneers of Iowan civilization — the vanguard of the mighty phalanx that is yet to come.

The immigration to Iowa reminds one of the legendary days of the Crusaders. As did the venturous knights of old, the emigrants resign the endearments and luxuries of home, to build up for themselves a glorious destiny, amid the wilds of a strange land. They go to rescue from the desolation entailed upon it by savage hordes, a region stored with Nature's lavish gifts; and, as those misled champions of the cross, they sally forth in banded numbers, from every point of a civilized world, to meet in the brotherhood of a great cause, on the fertile plains where tower their mutual hopes. But here the resemblance ends. The valiant knight of old went forth arrayed in all the paraphernalia of war, to conquer—to subdue—to win, by fire and sword, a land rich in historic lore — a land whose interest mainly lay in the hereditary annals of the past. But the modern emigrant wends his way to territories, whose history is yet unknown, whose annals are yet unwritten, whose value and grandeur lie in the promises of the future.—The plough-share and the pruning-hook are his weapons, his companions are the loved ones of either sex. The Crusader went to tear down—to demolish —a dynasty; the emigrant, to build up a State. The former had history for his guide — the latter had a history to frame and write.

And nobly has he written it. In the unexcelled prosperity of the land of his adoption — in the magic growth of her cities—upon her boundless prairies, as on a vast sheet—has he traced the records of Iowa's liberation from the darkness of the Indian ages. And these are records that posterity will read with pride, when the crumbling monument and mouldering legend of battle and of victory will be as "a tale of days forgotten."

IOWA — once the freehold of the tawny savage — is now a civilized and settled State. Where once the wolf went bounding, now waves the yellow corn; and where the owlet ooted to the solitude, the cabin-smoke is floating on the air. Wherever the highway winds, the ever-recurring marks of cheerful industry — of progress — of prosperity — greet the traveller's eye, till one is disposed to rank this State as cotemporary with many of her elder sisters. The immigrant is no longer called on to endure the vicissitudes, the hardships, and the dangers of a frontier life. At every step he meets civilization — in many places, finds improvements in the art of farming, such as he dreamed not of in his Eastern home; and often an old familiar face — a friend who had been a neigbor in years gone by — greets his arrival. Yet, be it not supposed that Iowa is *full*. Far from it; still within her vast domain lie millions of untilled acres — unentered — untouched — unreclaimed from primeval wildness. They await the immigrant — they call to him and bid him come. Shall it be asked what inducements they hold forth to tempt him, or what resources they possess to repay his labor? We ask, on the other hand, what do they not hold forth? The fertility of the soil in Iowa is unsurpassed—not merely by that of her kindred States — not merely in our Union—but throughout the world! The black loam that overlies her prairies, and which varies in depth from eighteen to forty-eight inches, forms an inexhaustible storehouse of fecundity and agricultural wealth. It rests upon a deep subsoil of clay, well fitted to retain moisture; and, during the driest portions of the year, this moisture reascends through the surface-muck—thus, by a constant reaction, weakening, if not annulling the effects of the severest drought. This was fully proved during the excessive aridity of 1854, Iowa having suffered less from its effects than any other State in the Union, and having, since then, been the granary of that Union, and supplied from her own stores the exhausted markets of the East and South. This may sound incredible — fabulous; and yet, Iowa, the youngest of the States, has actually accomplished it!

Such are the inducements Iowa holds out to the farmer, coupled with a promise to return him, for immeasurably less labor than would be required in the East, an unsurpassable abundance of any and every article which the zone we live in is capable of producing.

But again: to the manufacturer she also cries *come!* She invites him to behold for himself her immense coal regions, and examine the qualities of the coal; to roam, hand in hand with the farmer, over the vast mineral tracts; and while he admires the richness of the mines, to let the farmer wonder at the phenomenon of an exceedingly fertile soil, spread out upon the immense beds of lead. Nor is this all. — The abundance of first-rate water-power, and the amount of building-stone everywhere to be found, offer such advantages to the energetic manufacturer as he may elsewhere seek in vain.

These facts have but recently reached the East—and see with what avidity men of capital are hastening to test these boasted resources. And still the field is open—still the coffers of the earth are full, and he may help himself who will.

The poor and the lowly came a few years since, but now the rich and the lofty flock to Iowa, as well as they. And, thanks to the enterprise of these, the colossal wheel of manufacture has already been set in motion in Iowa. It revolves as yet but slowly, and its reverberating strokes do but send forth, as yet, prophetic echoes throughout the State, that tell what may—what *can and will be done.* When the Giant Spirit of Human Art shall have chained the flow of Iowa's great central artery, and assumed the directing of its course —when the Mississippi's waves shall foam and lash in their impeded progress — when the Missouri's waters shall be darkened by the shadows and the smoke of mammoth factories —and when the tributary streams of this great trio shall be made to join in this work of grandeur and of usefulness — then will that Giant Spirit, as he listens to the ponderous humming of that colossal wheel, whose accelerated revolutions will then keep time with the pulsations of Iowa's ambitious heart, find a genial home in the young, and promising, and vigorous State. There is in this picture no fiction —no visionary anticipation: all that we have hinted at, and more, will be realized. It requires no gift of prophecy to trace out the future path of Iowa. An observing eye — aided by a spirit of discrimination—need but take the past for a precedent—the present for an earnest—to draw a vast panorama of prosperity, such as our Union has perhaps never witnessed, heretofore, and yet, which Iowa will not fail to excel.

To the law-loving and the temperate — to the enterprising, the vigorous, the ambitious — she offers a home and a field worthy of their noblest efforts. Already has she placed the early adventurer on a throne of fortune, thus amply rewarding his courage. At this day she points to still loftier thrones and richer diadems, held in reserve as the prizes of fearless energy — or better still, throws open to the world her exhaustless stores of wealth, and seems to say, "Behold your reward!" And as the multitudinous throngs hasten toward these goals of promise—as they crowd with eager steps, and work with untiring hands—they find that far from becoming drained, her resources deepen and increase in proportion as they take from them — not merely keeping pace with their accumulating wants, but ever exceeding them; it is even as the province of mind — the realms of intellect— whose boundaries still widen, and whose sphere continues to expand, the further they are explored.

There is an emigration that thins the old and crowded States on the Atlantic seaboard; there is an immigration that peoples a new world, and darkens the mountain-slope of fortune; there is a journeying from the old into the new, of the Pilgrims of Industry and of Hope. But there is a mightier emigration—a vaster pilgrimage—than these. It is the march, onward and upward into the Future, of Iowa herself. As the immigrant mother leads her sons and daughters into the undeveloped paths of wealth—as civilization elevates a race out of the sloughs of semi-barbarism—as national prosperity exalts a land—or as science raises the human intellect from darkness into dazzling light—thus Iowa, with rapid strides, ascends the precipitous sides of prosperity's mountain-range, bearing her sons and daughters to loftier, and still loftier peaks, and revealing to their gaze still wider and richer vistas. And the summit of this range she will *never* reach; for her onward progress cannot be stayed, until her arterial streams are dry—until the agricultural life-blood in her veins has ceased to flow, until her great metallic heart has been emptied. Upon the topmost summit, then, Iowa will never stand, for through countless ages yet to come, her progress—that must be forever onward—must be upward also.

INTRODUCTION

TO THE SECOND EDITION.

The rapid growth of the State of Iowa, in population and importance, the increasing interest in her agricultural, mineralogical, and geological resources, manifested by the eagerness with which thousands daily hasten thitherward, as well as by the unprecedented sale of the first edition of this work, seems to demand, that if the author would correctly portray to the world "Iowa as it is," he must revise, correct, and enlarge, or issue an entire new volume, at least once a year; hence the present edition appears before you.

This edition has undergone a thorough revision and correction. The subject-matter and statistics relative to every particular county in the State, are correct, up to the 1st of February, 1856. By reference to the Table of Contents, it will be seen we have added chapters on Agriculture, times of holding Courts, a complete list of Post Offices in the State, and much other valuable information not in print elsewhere.

In the beginning, we felt that such a work was needed, and the avidity with which it has been sought by the westward-moving masses, and by all classes of every State, has corroborated that belief. We have devoted much of the past year in procuring facts and statistics, which we herein publish.

Confident in the correctness of its statements, and anticipating a like result from its issue, we ask for *this* the very liberal patronage extended to our first edition.

N. H. P.

Clinton, Iowa, *March* 1, 1856.

IOWA AS IT IS.

CHAPTER I.

EARLY HISTORY AND ACCESSION OF TERRITORY—ORGANIZATION — BOUNDARIES, AREA, ETC.

FOR centuries past, until the year 1830, the Northwestern Territory, embracing all lands west of the Mississippi, of which Iowa is now a part, was in the undisputed possession of various tribes of Indians; and the cultivated fields of the open prairie, the bluff-site of the magnificent residence, the ground upon which are now erected our halls of justice and houses of worship, was, but a few short years since, the battle-fields of numerous Indian tribes, contending for the possession of this beautiful and fertile soil, upon which each so freely shed the blood of their contending foes. The hills, valleys, rivers, and prairies of Iowa, have witnessed the most bloody conflicts ever fought by the savages of this continent, as the numerous bone-strewn battle-fields well testify.*

* The fertile plains of our present Iowa were first discovered in 1673, by a French exploring expedition from Canada, and were

The territory embraced within the bounds of Iowa has been purchased by four different treaties. The first was made in 1832—commonly called "the Black-Hawk Purchase;" the second in 1836, the third in 1837, and the fourth and last in 1842.

The oldest settlement in the State is Dubuque; which, as a trading-post, is identified with the Frenchman whose name it perpetuates. At about the same period, in 1832, Galena was a village, and Fort Madison and Bellevue military posts. Early in the spring of 1833, several companies of whites crossed from Illinois into Iowa in the vicinity of Burlington. From this period the progress and extension of settlements have been rapid, and the population has increased with greater rapidity than in the history of previous territories.

In 1834, Congress attached this Territory to that of Michigan for temporary jurisdiction, and two large counties—Dubuque and Des Moines—were organized. Their aggregate population in 1836 was 1053; and during the same year Wisconsin was organized as a separate Territory, and exercised jurisdiction over "the District of Iowa."

The "Territory of Iowa" was organized on the 4th of July, 1838. Robert Lucas, a former Governor of Ohio, was Governor and Superintendent of Indian Affairs of the new Territory. During that year, the State was subdivided into sixteen counties, and contained a population of 22,860.

The first Legislature held in Iowa met at Burlington, in

---

then the home of the Dacotahs, who were the terror of their savage neighbors.

the fall of 1837, while our State was attached to Wisconsin, yet subject to Michigan in judicial matters.

On the 4th of July, 1838, Iowa was separated from Wisconsin by Act of Congress, passed June 12th, 1838.

In 1839, the General Assembly located the Seat of Government on the Iowa River, and called the place the "City of Iowa."

In 1843, the Territorial Legislature petitioned Congress for authority to adopt a State Constitution; which was granted at the next session; and on the 7th of October, 1844, the Convention assembled and adopted a Constitution, which was not approved by Congress. A second Convention was held in 1846, the limits restricted, an amended Constitution adopted; this was submitted to Congress and approved; and in December, 1846, the "State of Iowa" was admitted and christened as one of the glorious Confederacy.

The State of Iowa is situated between 40° 30′ and 43° 30′ north latitude, and between 90° 20′ and 97° 40′ west longitude; is bounded on the north by Minnesota Territory, east by the Mississippi River (which separates it from Wisconsin and Illinois), south by Missouri, and west by the Missouri River (which separates it from Nebraska Territory). The State contains an area of 56,000 square miles; being upwards of 200 miles wide from north to south, and upwards of 300 long from east to west. The State is divided into one hundred counties; eighty-five of which have been surveyed, and seventy regularly organized.

CHAPTER II.

THE CLIMATE.

We have, generally, an unbroken winter from the middle of November till January, when we are almost invariably visited with a "January thaw;" after which the weather is generally mild, and gradually merges into spring. We are free from the sudden changes of New-England, and from the long drizzling rains and foggy weather of portions of the Middle States. But Iowa, in common with other States, must except tho prolonged intense cold weather of last winter.

This State is located in the healthiest latitude of our continent; reaching only to latitude 43° 30′ on its northern boundary. Its winters are comparatively mild and pleasant, and its summers free from the long scorching rays of a southern sun and the epidemics so common in such climates.* By the medical journals, Iowa is ranked as

* Dr. Updegraff, a correspondent of the *Ohio Farmer*, thus alludes to our climate, &c.:

"Of all other considerations respecting a new country, the most important is as to its *healthiness.*

"In this respect, Iowa has the advantage of most new countries. An open prairie country, almost universally rolling, or even *hilly*, it is more favorable to health than flat prairie or level woodland. The streams are mostly fresh running water, with sandy or gravel beds. The scarcity of timber-land, and the annual fires that pass over the prairies, prevent, to a great degree, second only in point of health; and no doubt it will be *first*, when she has a settled and acclimated population, as free from toil, privations, and exposure as other states.

One of the peculiarities of this climate is the dryness of its summers and autumns. A drought often commences in August, which, with the exception of a few showers towards the close of that month, continues, with little interruption, throughout the fall season. The autumnal months are almost invariably clear, warm, and dry. The immense mass of vegetation with which this fertile soil loads itself during the summer is suddenly withered, and the whole earth is covered with combustible materials. This is especially true of those portions where grass grows from two to ten feet high, and is exposed to sun and wind, becoming thoroughly dried. A single spark of fire, falling upon the prairie at such a time, instantly kindles a blaze that spreads on every side, and continues its destructive course as long as it finds fuel. These fires sweep along with great power and rapidity, and frequently extend across a wide prairie and advance in a long line. No sight can be more sublime than a stream of fire, beheld at night, several miles in

---

the decomposition of vegetable matter; which is, in most new countries, the great source of disease. With some local exceptions, there does not seem to be any natural reason why this State, even in its early settlement, should not enjoy as high an *average* of healthiness as Ohio *now* does. Such I believe to be the fact, after making proper deductions for change of climate, mode of life, exposure, and unusual exertion. To observe the exertion and exposure, often reckless and unnecessary, to which most new settlers subject themselves, it becomes a matter of surprise that disease and mortality are not much more usual than they are."

breadth, advancing across the plains, leaving behind it a background of dense black smoke, throwing before it a vivid glare, which lights up the whole landscape for miles with the brilliancy of noonday. These fires are so thorough in their progress, that they destroy every combustible before them. The roots of the prairie-grass, and several species of flowers, however, by some peculiar adaptation of nature, are spared.

A narrow strip of bare ground, or a beaten road, the width of a common wagon-track, will prevent the fire from extending beyond it; yet careless, thoughtless farmers, sometimes suffer tall grass to connect their fields of corn and fences with the wild prairie, and forfeit their year's toil as a penalty for their slothfulness!

CHAPTER III.

THE SOIL.

It is well known to the scientific farmer, that the land best suited to wheat and most small grains, and in which the earthy, saline, and organic matters are distributed in the proportion best adapted to impart fertility and durability, is generally a soil based on the calcareous and magnesio-calcareous rocks. This condition particularly characterizes the country bordering on the Mississippi and its tributaries, between the 41st and 45th degrees of latitude, which has an average width of 20 to 30 miles west of the line of that river. In this State, it includes the Dubuque District, the country watered by the Des Moines, and the two Iowas. In *Owen's Geological Report*, we find the following:

"The prairie country, based on rocks belonging to the Devonian and carboniferous systems, extending up the valley of the Red Cedar, Iowa, and Des Moines, as high as latitude 42° 31′, presents a body of arable land which, taken as a whole, for richness and organic elements, for amount of saline matter, and due admixture of earthy silicates, affords a combination that belongs only to the most fertile upland plains. Throughout this district the general levelness of the surface, interrupted only by gentle swells and moderate undulations, offers facilities for the introduction of all those aids which machinery is daily adding to diminish the labor of cultivation, and render easy and expeditious the collection of an abundant harvest."

Again, in speaking of the physical and agricultural character of the State, bordering on the Mississippi, Owen says:

"The carboniferous rocks of Iowa occupy a region of country which, taken as a whole, is one of the most fertile in the United States. No country can present to the farmer greater facilities for subduing, in a short time, wild land. Its native prairies are fields, almost ready made to his hands. Its rich, black soil, scarcely less productive than that of the Cedar Valley, returns him reward for his labor a hundredfold. The only drawback to its productiveness is that, on some of the higher grounds, the soil, partaking of the mixed character common to drift-soils, is occasionally gravelly, and that, here and there, when the upper members of the coal-measures prevail, it becomes somewhat too siliceous.

"The future farms of Iowa, large, level, and unbroken by stump or other obstruction, will afford an excellent field for the introduction of mowing-machines, and other improved implements calculated to save the labor of the husbandman, and which, in new countries, reclaimed from the forest, can scarcely be employed until the first generation shall have passed away.

Since "a tree is known by its fruits," and the soil by its yield, we mention a few items, showing the results of the tiller's toil, in some parts of Iowa, in 1855, which will give some idea of the fertility of our soil.

Robert Rawlins, of Washington county, exhibited 8 stalks of corn, 11 feet high, bearing 11 ears, 10 rows on each ear, and 47 grains to a row, making 88 feet of stalk, and 5170 grains of plump white corn, *the produce of a single grain!* Messrs. Harrow, of Wapello county, exhibited specimens from a field which produced the extraordinary yield of *one hundred and sixty-eight bushels of corn per acre!* Jerome Parsons, of Jefferson county, exhibited specimens of red-chaff bearded wheat, from the almost unprecedented yield of *forty-seven bushels to the acre!*

Of potatoes, raised in Jefferson county, 105 bushels to the acre: some specimens 9 by 16 inches in circumference. Of beets, 27 inches in length; and others 31 in circumference, weighing 17 lbs. Squashes in Western Iowa, weighing 100 lbs.; also, in Northern Iowa, a squash vine 275 feet long, bearing, among others, 5 squashes which average 80 lbs. each, all from one seed! Mr. Elisha Pierson, near Iowa City, raised over half a ton of squashes from two seeds! One of his yield weighed 139 lbs., and measured 7 feet 2 inches in circumference, and the smallest weighed 100 lbs. We have seen apples weighing 24 ounces each, and pears of 28 ounces weight each.

More full and minute descriptions of the soil in various localities in the State may be found in the series of articles upon "the Counties and Towns of Iowa," and in the Agricultural chapter.

CHAPTER IV.

GENERAL APPEARANCE OF THE PRAIRIES.

THE novelty of the prairie country is striking, and never fails to cause an exclamation of surprise from those who have lived amid the forests of Ohio and Kentucky, or along the wooded shores of the Atlantic, or in sight of the rocky barriers of the Allegheny ridge. The extent of the prospect is exhilarating. The outline of the landscape is undulating and graceful. The verdure and the flowers are beautiful; and the absence of shade, and consequent appearance of a profusion of light, produces a gaiety which animates every beholder.

These plains, although preserving a general level in respect to the whole country, are yet, in themselves, *not flat*, but exhibit a gracefully waving surface, swelling and sinking with easy, graceful slopes, and full, rounded outlines, equally avoiding the unmeaning horizontal surface, and the interruption of abrupt or angular elevations.

The attraction of the prairie consists in its extent, its carpet of verdure and flowers, its undulating surface, its groves, and the fringe of timber by which it is surrounded. Of all of these, the latter is the most expressive feature. It is that which gives character to the landscape, which imparts the shape, and marks the boundary of the plain. If the prairie be small, its greatest beauty consists in the vicinity of the surrounding margin of woodland, which resembles the shore of a lake indented with deep vistas, like bays and inlets, and throwing out long points, like capes and headlands.

In the spring of the year, when the young grass has just covered the ground with a carpet of delicate green, and especially if the sun is rising from behind a distant swell of the plain and glittering upon the dewdrops, no scene can be more lovely to the eye. The groves, or clusters of timber, are particularly attractive at this season of the year. The rich undergrowth is in full bloom. The rosewood, dogwood, crab-apple, wild plum, the cherry, and the wild rose are all abundant, and in many portions of the State the grape-vine abounds. The variety of wild fruit and flowering shrubs is so great, and such the profusion of the blossoms with which they are bowed down, that the eye is regaled almost to satiety.

The gaiety of the prairie, its embellishments, and the absence of the gloom and savage wildness of the forest, all contribute to dispel the feeling of loneliness which usually creeps over the mind of the solitary traveller in the wilderness. Though he may not see a house or a human being, and is conscious that he is far from the habitations of men, the traveller upon the prairie can scarcely divest himself of the idea that he is travelling through scenes embellished by the hand of art. The flowers, so fragile, so delicate, and so ornamental, seem to have been tastefully disposed to adorn the scene.

In the summer, the prairie is covered with long, coarse grass, which soon assumes a golden hue, and waves in the wind like a fully ripe harvest. The prairie-grass never attains its highest growth in the richest soil; but in low, wet, or marshy land, where the substratum of clay lies near the surface, the centre or main stem of the grass — that which bears the seed—shoots up to the height of eight and ten feet, throwing out long, coarse leaves or blades. But on the rich, undulating prairies, the grass is finer, with less of stalk and a greater profusion of leaves. The roots spread and interweave, forming a compact, even sod, and the blades expand into a close, thick grass, which is seldom more than eighteen inches high, until late in the season, when the seed-bearing stem shoots up. The first coat is mingled with small flowers — the violet, the bloom of the wild strawberry, and various others, of the most minute and delicate texture. As the grass increases in height, these smaller flowers disappear, and others, taller and more gaudy, display their brilliant colors upon the green surface; and still later, a larger and coarser succession arises with the rising tide of verdure. It is impossible to conceive a more infinite diversity, or a richer profusion of hues, "from grave to gay," than graces the beautiful carpet of green throughout the entire season of summer.

When the prairie is bare, it is easy to distinguish the rich from the poorer lands, by the small hillocks which are cattered over them, and which are most abundant where the soil is least productive. They are from a few inches to two or three feet in height, and only exist where the clay lies near the surface; as such mounds composed of rich mould would soon crumble and become level. These, by some, are said to be the work of the *gophor* — a small quadruped; by others, are thought to be thrown up by *craw-fish;* which is doubtless true of wet situations; while those in drier portions are attributed to colonies of ants: each class belonging, however, to the clay party, and working only in poor soil.

CHAPTER V.

IOWA SCENERY — THE BLUFFS, ETC.

RESPECTING the scenery of Iowa, Owen, in his Geological Report to Congress, pp. 64, 65, and 66, says:

"The scenery on the Rhine, with its castellated heights, has furnished many of the most favorite subjects for the artist's pencil, and been the admiration of European travellers for centuries. Yet it is doubtful whether, in actual beauty of landscape, it is not equalled by that of some of the streams that water this region of the Far West. It is certain that, though the rock formations essentially differ, Nature has here fashioned, on an extensive scale, and in advance of all civilization, remarkable and curious counterparts to the artificial landscape which has given celebrity to that part of the European Continent.

"The features of the scenery are not, indeed, of the loftiest and most impressive character — such as one might expect to witness on approaching the source of one of the two largest rivers on the globe. There are no elevated peaks, rising in majestic grandeur; no mountain torrents, shrouded in foam, and chafing in their rocky channels; no deep and narrow valleys, hemmed in on every side, and forming, as it were, a little world of their own; no narrow and precipitous passes, winding through circuitous defiles; no cavernous gorges, giving exit to pent-up waters; no contorted and twisted strata, affording evidence of gigantic and violent throes. But the features of the scene, though less grave and bold than those of mountainous regions, are yet impressive and strongly marked. We find the luxuriant sward, clothing the hill-slope even down to the water's edge. We have the steep cliff, shooting up through its mural escarpments. We have the stream, clear as crystal, now quiet, and smooth, and glassy, then ruffled by a temporary rapid; or, when a terrace of rock abruptly crosses it, broken up into a small, romantic cascade. We have clumps of trees, disposed with an effect that might baffle the landscape gardener; now crowning the grassy height, now dotting the green slope with partial and isolated shade. From the hill-tops, the intervening valleys wear the aspect of cultivated meadows and rich pasture-grounds, irrigated by frequent rivulets, that wend their way through fields of wild hay fringed with flourishing willows. Here and there, occupying its nook on the bank of the stream, at some favorable spot, occurs the solitary wigwam, with its scanty appurtenances. On the summit-level spreads the wide prairie, decked with flowers of the gayest hue; its long, undulating waves, stretching away till sky and meadow mingle in the distant horizon. The whole combination suggests the idea, not of an aboriginal wilderness (so recently), inhabited by savage tribes, but of a country lately under a high state of cultivation, and suddenly deserted by its inhabitants — their dwellings, indeed, gone, but the castle-homes of their chieftains only partially destroyed, and showing, in ruins, on the rocky summits around. This latter feature, especially, aids the delusion; for the peculiar aspect of the exposed limestone, and its manner of weathering, cause it to assume a semblance somewhat fantastic, indeed, but yet wonderfully close and faithful to the dilapidated wall, with its crowning parapet, and its projecting buttresses, and its flanking towers, and even the lesser details that mark the fortress of the olden time."

"The rural beauty of this portion of Iowa can hardly be surpassed. Undulating prairies, interspersed with open groves of timber, and watered with pebbly or rocky-bedded streams, pure and transparent; hills of moderate height and gentle slope; here and there, especially towards the heads of streams, small lakes, as clear as the rivers, some

Hills of Silicious Marl, Council Bluffs.

skirted with timber, some with banks formed by the greensward of the open prairie. These are the ordinary features of the pastoral landscape."

In a few instances, the hills or bluffs along the Mississippi rise boldly from the water's edge, or push out their steep promontories, so as to change the direction of the river; but more generally, on either bank of the river, we see a series of graceful slopes, swelling and sinking as far as the eye can reach. The prairie, for the most part extending to the water's edge, renders the scenery truly beautiful. Imagine a stream a mile in width, whose waters are as transparent as those of the mountain spring, flowing over beds of rock and gravel; fancy the prairie commencing at the water's edge—a natural meadow of deep-green grass and beautiful and fragrant flowers, rising with a gentle slope for miles, so that, in the vast panorama, thousands of acres are exposed to the eye. The prospect is bounded by a range of low hills, which sometimes approach the river, and again recede, and whose summits, which are seen gently waving along the horizon, form the level of the adjacent country. Sometimes the woodland extends along this river for miles continuously; again, it stretches in a wide belt far off into the country, marking the course of some tributary streams; and sometimes, in vast groves, several miles in extent, standing alone, like islands in this wilderness of grass and flowers.

CHAPTER VI.

RIVERS AND THEIR TRIBUTARIES.

No State in the Union is more bountifully supplied with water than Iowa; being bounded on the east by one of the finest rivers in the world — the Mississippi, and on the west by the Missouri; the interior of the State being traversed in every direction by noble, and in many cases navigable, streams; many of them running parallel to each other, from twelve to twenty miles apart, skirted with timber of from one to five miles in width. Our rivers have not the rapidity of the New-England streams, nor the depth and sluggishness of those of the South; but are clear, fresh, and healthy, of gentle current, and capable of furnishing water-power for all purposes.

The rivers that are directly tributary to the Mississippi are the Upper Iowa, Turkey, Maquoketa, Wapsipinnicon, Cedar, Iowa, Fox, Checaque (commonly called Skunk), and the Des Moines. Those running into the Missouri are Floyd's, Little Sioux, Inyan Yankee, Soldier, Boyer, Nishnabotna, Big Tarkeo, and Nodaway.

Some of these streams are navigable for a great distance, and the day is drawing nigh when the quiet of their banks shall be broken, and the shrill whistle of the heavily-laden steamer reverberate from shore to shore — when many of these streams shall have become thoroughfares for the transportation of the rich productions of this most fertile and most prosperous State. "The untold powers of some of these waters will soon be utilized for mechanical purposes; and but a short time will elapse ere the thunder and clatter of the ten thousand wheels of machinery will break upon that solitude which now echoes only to the harvest-song or the notes of the sweet warblers of the forest. Extensive works are already commenced upon more than one of these rivers which will stamp our greatness and convince the world that 'progress' is our watchword."

Besides those mentioned, are their tributaries — the creeks, branches, or rivulets, penetrating every portion of the interior of the State; springs of clear, cold water, also abound in all parts of the State. [Particular reference is made to the sites for water-power in different locations, in the letters from county-seats, in another portion of this work.]

CHAPTER VII.

TIMBER-LANDS.

To the farmer from the forests of any of the Middle or Eastern States, who has spent years of most laborious and painful drudgery in "clearing up" his land, and with whom the most desirable object has been the *destruction* of timber, the scarcity of it here seems an evil without a remedy. But we contend that that which appears to the superficial observer as a defect, is, in truth, one of the greatest sources of prosperity in our country.

Let us contrast life in "the wooden country" with a life here upon the wide prairie. The labor of clearing woodland is the most arduous task to which the farmer is subjected; and frequently the new-comer from the East, who settles in the forests of Ohio and Kentucky, consumes years of painful toil, and wastes the prime of life, before he sees the fruits of his labor. Besides, the industry and trade of the country are not enhanced, because those who are clearing new land cannot for years produce anything for market. Again, the clearing of new lands suddenly exposes the vegetable deposits of ages to the glaring beams of the sun; which, with the thousands of fallen and rotting trees, fill the air with noxious exhalations, producing diseases of the most malignant character.

Quite different is the case in our open prairie country. The settler may always select upon the prairie, land as fertile as the richest river-bottoms; and, by settling on the edge of the timber, combine every advantage afforded by the latter. The land being already cleared, he has only to enclose and break it. The sod (described in another section) is turned over with a heavy plow and strong team. The corn is dropped in the furrows, covered with a hoe, and thus left to be gathered. Several other modes of corn-planting may be worthy of mention; one of which is performed by striking an axe into the sod and dropping the corn into the crevice; another, by dropping the corn in every fourth row in plowing, which is covered by the plowing of the fifth. Thus, while the overturned sod is undergoing decomposition, and becoming mellow by exposing the fibrous roots to the sun, it is also affording nourishment to the growing corn. Neither the yield nor the grain is very good the first season; but sufficient to reward amply the labor of planting and gathering. By the ensuing spring, the roots of the wild grass are completely rotted, and the rich, light mould, unencumbered with rocks and stumps, is fit for all the purposes of husbandry. The plow, running easily through the rich, loamy soil, can be as well managed by a half-grown boy as the strongest plowman.

Thus, it is seen, the difference in the greater facility of working prairie-lands, the saving in the wear of farming utensils, the economy of time, and greater degree of certainty in the farmer's calculations, and the enjoyment of health, more than outweigh any inconvenience which can possibly be experienced in this country from the want of timber, even under the most unfavorable circumstances.

"According to the most reliable estimates, about *one-tenth* of Iowa is timber-land. Of this a considerable portion is of inferior quality; and the supply of the finest growth of timber, such as we find in Ohio, is comparatively small. Yet along the streams there are thousands of acres covered with an excellent growth of oak, walnut, ash, linn maple, hickory, elm, and cotton-wood. These varieties differ in different localities. Along the Iowa and Cedar Rivers, there is a large amount of oak of all varieties; and the valleys of the Des Moines are abundantly supplied with walnut. Hickory and walnut are abundant on the Iowa,

Skunk, Cedar, and other rivers. Besides the full-grown timber, there are thousands of acres of a vigorous young growth, that has at last conquered the prairie fires, and is now rapidly coming to maturity. In addition to these, there is a vast amount of locust being cultivated. This grows here with a rapidity that is seldom equalled elsewhere. I have seen trees at the age of ten years that would make eight posts of sufficient size for fencing. Thus there is an abundance of timber for present purposes, and it is believed by those best informed, that, notwithstanding the constant demand, the supply is every day increasing, both from natural and cultivated sources.

"The unequal distribution of the wooded land is a greater objection than its actual quantity. Sometimes the prairies are from twenty to forty miles in width, thus making timber inconvenient. These, however, are rare cases, and, at the worst, are bearable, compared to the life-long drudgery of woodland pioneering.

"The large amount of coal that is now discovered in the various sections of the State obviate, to a great extent, the limited supply of timber-land. The rapidly-increasing facilities for inter-communication are also fast equalizing the advantages of different localities. It is not the economy of nature that any one spot should monopolize all natural advantages; but some portions of this appear to combine as many as are often found harmonizing."

The portion of Iowa most deficient in timber is north of latitude 42°—especially on dividing ridges. North of this latitude, between the head-waters of Three and Grand

Rivers, there are distances of ten and fifteen miles without any timber; while between the waters of Grand River, the Nodaway, and the Nishnabotna, the open prairie is often twenty miles wide, without a bush to be seen higher than the wild indigo and the compass plant.

CHAPTER VIII.

GEOLOGY OF IOWA.

IN preparing the following, we depend in part upon "Owen's Geological Report" of a survey made under his direction, of the Northwest Territory, by authority of Congress.

Minerals.

The principal minerals of Iowa are lead, iron, and copper. The shipment of lead from Dubuque, from the 21st of March to the 1st of December, 1854, inclusive, amounted to 43,543 pigs, weighing 3,069,640 lbs.; valued, at the mines, $178,830,20. Lead has been found at various other places near the base of a bluff on the west side of the Mississippi, some ten or fifteen miles above Turkey River, near the French village. From seven to ten thousand pounds of lead ore were taken from openings in the rocks by Dr. Andrus. More or less "Galena" is found here in all the principal openings for the distance of a mile. Between the Yellow and Upper Iowa Rivers, excavations are visible where the Indians have dug for lead ore. On the Upper Iowa, also, ore has been discovered in several places in considerable quantities. In the Winnebago Reserve, not far from the Iowa River, and a few miles northwest of the town of Lansing, lead ore has been found in small quantities, chiefly in pockets and cavities.

Copper ore has been discovered within the boundaries of the State, but not sufficiently productive to justify the sinking of shafts. Iron ore is found in various places in the Des Moines Valley; Owen thought, in some locations, of sufficient productiveness to justify smelting. There are, as yet, no works for working raw iron ore in the State.

Coal-fields of Iowa.

Last summer, the following article appeared in the *Des Moines Valley Whig.* Having compared it with other authority, we find it quite correct, and insert it entire, with additional data, gathered elsewhere, as a condensed view of Iowa coal measures, &c.:

"The Des Moines River runs centrally and diagonally through what is geologically called the Carboniferous System of Iowa. This system is called carboniferous, because it is that particular division of rocks in which the 'coal measures' are found, and because it contains that series of rocks, of a comparatively modern date, which, in their composition, are so largely carbon.

"The physical and pastoral features of the Des Moines Valley are thus given in Owen's Geological Survey:

"'The carboniferous rocks of Iowa occupy a region of

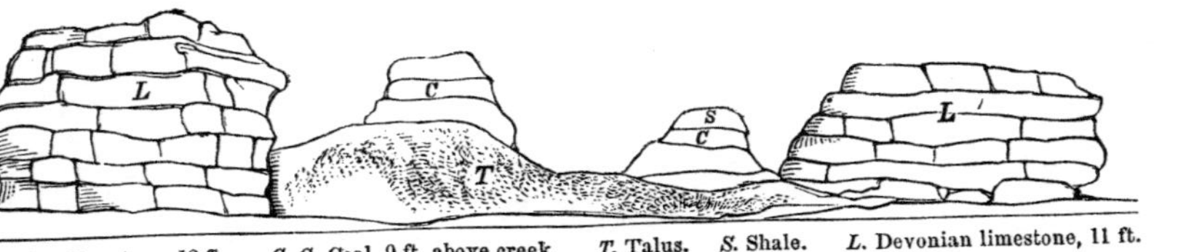

L. Devonian limestone, 18 ft. *C, C.* Coal, 9 ft. above creek. *T.* Talus. *S.* Shale. *L.* Devonian limestone, 11 ft.

SECTION ON CREEK NEAR ROCKINGHAM, SCOTT COUNTY, SHOWING OUT-CROP OF COAL.

country which, taken as a whole, is one of the most fertile in the United States. No country can present to the farmer greater facilities for subduing, in a short time, wild land.

"'For centuries the succession of natural crops of grass, untouched by the scythe, and but very partially kept down by the pasturage of buffalo and other herbivorous animals, have accumulated organic matter on the surface-soil to such an extent that a large succession, even of exhausting crops, will not materially impoverish the land.

"'The rural beauty of this portion of Iowa can hardly be surpassed. Undulating prairies, interspersed with open groves of timber, and watered by pebbly or rocky-bedded streams, pure and transparent; hills of moderate height and gentle slope; here and there, especially towards the heads of the streams, small lakes, as clear as the rivers, some skirted with timber, some with banks formed by the greensward of the open prairie; these are the ordinary features of the pastoral landscape.' (Report, p. 100.)

"The principal minerals to be noticed in this paper are coal, hydraulic limestone, quartzite, clays, common or mountain limestone, marble, iron ore, and gypsum.

Coal.

The Iowa Coal-field embraces an area of about 25,000 square miles. A very good idea of its locality may be obtained by taking a map and drawing a line, commencing near the southwest corner of the State, proceeding up the Nishnabotna; thence to Lake Boyer; thence, by the heads of the Three Rivers, northeast, to the Des Moines, crossing it six miles above Fort Dodge; thence southeast, through Tama and Iowa Counties, to the east part of Washington County; thence nearly south, through the west part of Henry and Lee Counties, to the Des Moines River, near St. Francisville. It is nearly in the shape of a half ellipse, cut by the shortest diameter. The width of it east and west is nearly 200 miles; while in a north and south direction, the distance is 140 miles. The Des Moines River traverses, in a southeast direction, about 250 miles.

The accompanying table has, with much care and some labor, been compiled from Owen's Report, for the purpose of giving a view of the thickness of the coal veins as they show themselves in the Valley proper, and in the banks of creeks near by:

Tabular View of the Coal Beds in the Des Moines Valley.

Counties.	Range.		Section.	Veins.		General Remarks.
	N.	W.		Ft.	In.	
Lee	66	9	23	1		Quality poor.
Clark, Mo.......	67	8	36	3		Quality good.
Van Buren......	68	8	24	4	6	Night's Bank, good.
"	68	8	34	4		Regular 4 to 5 feet.
"	68	8	25·26	2		Slaughter's Bank.
"	69	8 & 9	32	2		On Bear Creek.
"	69	9	25	1	6	Gillis's Bank.
"	70	11	3	4		Near Portland.
Davis.............	70	12	22	2		2 seams, 2 feet each.
Wapello	72	13		3		5 feet higher, 18 in.
"	73	15	20			Not given.
Mahaska	74	15	19·30	4		Quality tolerable.
"	74	17	6	3		
"	74	17	32	2	6	

Counties.	RANGE.		Section.	Veins.		General Remarks.
	N.	W.		Ft.	In.	
Marion	74	18	2	2		Right bank Cedar.
"	74	18	12	3		
"	74	18	16	5		
"	74	18	30			Regular 4 to 6 feet.
"	74	18	14	2		2½ feet poor.
"	75	20	3	3		White br'st ex.
"	76	19	14·23	4		" "
"	76	19	11			Not given.
Polk	78	23	23			" "
"	78	24	4	2		Regular 2 to 3 feet.
Boone	81	25				2 to 3 feet inferior.
"	83	26	5			Not given.

NOTE.—Last bed mentioned in latitude 42° 30′ north.'

The foregoing table does not include the thinnest veins, nor half the localities where the thick ones crop out; but one can get a very correct view of the thickness of the best seams up along the Valley. There are undoubtedly outcrops where the thickness is much greater than in any of the places mentioned. But these will be found to be the centre or side of a basin which, on being worked, will not extend far. A basin of 15 feet of thickness has been found in a bank opposite Farmington. Where the outcrops are more than four or five feet, they must be suspected as being basins, unless in the cut of a stream at some distance the vein is ascertained to have the same thickness. Owen says there is no vein of more than from four to five feet in Iowa. (Report, p. 20.)

The table shows outcrops are far more numerous in some localities than in others. In the immediate vicinity of the river, where the limestones, which lie below the coal, make their appearance, the coal strata are usually wanting. This is the case at Bonaparte, Bentonsport, Keosauqua and Ottumwa. But in these the coal strata may be, and actually are, found in creeks at no great distance from the river; sometimes, even upon the bluffs.

The southeast and northwest parts of Van Buren County, the northeast part of Davis, the central part of Wapello, the southern part of Mahaska, and the southeastern and central parts of Marion, are rich in coal. But other portions of the same counties are not wanting. So far as can be learned from the table, and so far as the observation and knowledge of the writer extends, the heaviest beds are usually on the west side of the river. The best beds are also there. Some of these are also on the White Breast, Cedar, and Soap Creeks. The principal exception to this rule is in the southeast part of Van Buren County. Here it exists in great abundance on both sides of the river. It is equal in quality to any found below Marion County. Two veins are worked to considerable extent in connection; the two afford from 4½ to 5½ feet. On the west side of the river, it is said the two are separated by a vein of fire-clay, which thins out, and the coal veins converge as they recede from the river. These veins are shown in the cuts made by the creeks for miles in distance to the west. During the year ending with the current June, more than 100,000 bushels have been taken from three banks near Farmington, two of which are east of the river. Some of this has been conveyed by blacksmiths the distance of 75 miles into the State of Missouri. The greater part of it has been transported to different places by wagons.

Castellated Appearance of Lower Magnesian Limestone, Upper Iowa.

The average value of it at the bank is 6¼ cents per bushel. The value at the Mississippi, a distance of 30 miles, is 18 to 20 cents per bushel. Whenever the banks shall be well opened, and there are ready and convenient means of carriage, so that colliers can find regular employment, coal can be delivered on the banks of the Mississippi at a cost of 6 or 7 cents per bushel, and afford a better profit than at present. This is upon the supposition that it can be conveyed upon a railroad car here as cheap as in Kentucky, where the cost of transportation is one cent per bushel per 100 miles. And as to the amount of coal the Valley can supply, it is easy to ascertain it. Allowing a bushel to the cubic foot, one acre, with a two-feet vein, will give 87,120 bushels. With a four-feet vein, one acre will give 174,240 bushels. One hundred acres, with a four-feet vein, will yield 17,424,000 bushels. One square mile, with a four-feet vein, will yield 111,513,600 bushels. The transportation of this 100 miles, at one cent per bushel, would yield the snug purse of $1,115,136. And as the demand for coal would at once be increased to millions of bushels a year, if a railroad was constructed in the Valley, this mineral alone would afford quite an item of business and profit.

Hydraulic Limestone.

Of this kind of stone is formed a mortar which will set under water. It is essential for all masonry exposed to the water and to dampness. There are several varieties of it: one is called Septaria. This is found in the form of round or flattened balls, of various sizes. This is the kind from which the English prepare the celebrated Roman Cement. (Hitchcock's Geology, p. 20.) Comstock speaks of it also as 'Argillo-Ferruginous Limestone.' This, however, is another variety of cement-rock, and is, perhaps, the most common. It is called black calcareous rock, cement rock, and hydraulic limestone. In reference to the geological formations in the Valley, Owen says, 'The middle division of the Iowa Coal-field affords, at many localities, iron-stones of various qualities, associated frequently with hydraulic calcareous cement, which occurs either in the form of disconnected septaria, or regular beds.' (Report, p. 21.)

Cement rock is found both above and below the coal, but in the largest quantities above. The reader will find mention of it by consulting Owen's Report, pp. 112, 127; and more frequently still in that part of it which gives the geological structure between Fort Des Moines and Fort Dodge. It is a very common rock in the Valley; probably in every county on the River below Fort Dodge. In many places contiguous to the river in Davis County, there are strata of it several feet in thickness. The geological structure of the southeast and central parts of Marion County are just the same as in Davis. But as the series of rocks *above* the coal show, themselves more extensively above Racoon Fork, we accordingly find more frequent mention of it in that region. In some places large quantities of it are wrought into cement, which is quite extensively used in the river improvement. The initials of it by analysis are:

"Carbonate of lime	63·6
Silica	15·5
Alumina	8·3
Protoxide of iron	7·4
Magnesia	1·2

With a small portion of manganese, soda, and potash.

It will readily be seen that the demand for this is great, when it is said that $6000 worth, at the ordinary prices, will be wanted for every lock on the river, and when it is also said that in nearly every dwelling in the western country, cistern coated with this cement will be indispensable as the means of obtaining a supply of pure, soft water. The walls and floors of damp cellars must also be laid in cement. And the cement of this Valley will be wanted because it is more accessible; the present demand being supplied, in a great measure, from La Salle, Illinois, and from Louisville, Kentucky; and also because the Valley cement is probably fully equal to that from other places. That the reader may see how its constituents compare with other cement, we will give the analysis of that which is extensively used in the State of New York. Its composition, according to Professor Beck, is:

Carbonate of lime	50·70
Silica	15·37
Alumina	9·13
Peroxide of iron	2·25
Magnesia	12·35

Comparing this analysis with that of the Valley cement, it will be seen that they are substantially the same. We will here add a practical remark, which may be of much value to those who undertake to manufacture this cement, and to those who undertake to test specimens. Very much depends upon burning it. If care be not taken, the best cement may be easily spoiled. In St. John's Geology, p. 274, will be found the following:

'Greater caution is requisite in burning hydraulic lime, since it is fusible, and the heat applied to the common lime will vitrify this substance and render the process quite imperfect. Common lime will bear a white heat; but the calcination of hydraulic lime is not well effected above a red heat.'

When proper arrangements shall be made for working this limestone, it is said the cement can be afforded at the kiln for $1·25 per barrel. The carriage of it to the Mississippi by land is at most $1·00 per barrel per 100 miles; while cement from other places costs from $3·00 to $3·50 per barrel.

Common Limestone.

Though this is regarded as prevailing rock in the West, there are large sections in Iowa where the limestone is so largely magnesian as to be unfit for quick-lime and mortar The proper position of the common or mountain limestone in the carboniferous system is below the coal. Accordingly, it is found all along the Valley in the greatest abundance and of the best quality. Much of it contains 90 per cent. of carbonate of lime. This is among the most valuable of stones for quick-lime.

Closely allied to this stone, and still lower in the system, is the blue lime-stone. Some of this is deep blue, and some, of a bluish gray. It is harder than common limestone, often highly crystalline, and fossiliferous. It usually lies in strata in the Valley, varying from a few inches to some feet in thickness. The stone is good for quick-lime, but is of superior quality for building material. It is as beautiful and durable as Quincy granite, while the cost of putting it into the wall is comparatively trifling. The principal places where it is accessible are Keokuk, in the bed of the river below Farmington, Keosauqua, and Outumwa. It will undoubtedly become an article of export as soon as it shall become known, when a demand for the best building material arises, and the proper means of transportation are provided.

Marble.

The writer claims that there is marble in the Des Moines Valley, of a good quality and in great quantity. 'Any limestone which is sufficiently hard to take a fine polish is called marble. Many of these are fossiliferous.' (Lyell's Elements of Geology, p. 12.) In the limestones beneath the coal there are several varieties which come under this definition. Among them may be classed some of those named under the previous head. The best quarry now known in the Valley is at Keokuk. Some of the strata there are highly crystalline—almost saccharine—and take a fine polish. St. Louis has already resorted to this place for building material; a fact which shows that this marble is superior to any other equally accessible to that city. At the same locality are other varieties which polish well. They are crystalline, solid, but full of fossils, and either blue, or of a bluish-gray color. Of the latter varieties, enough can be had at Bonaparte, Bentonsport, and Keosauqua. And very probably, when these quarries shall be extensively worked, the white marble will be found.

Not far from Keosauqua there is a good variety of light-gray, compact, granular marble, of which tomb-stones are wrought by Deacon M. B. Root. It effervesces slightly with acids, and takes a polish. Iowa sent a block from this quarry to the Washington Monument. Ottumwa may expect to find as good varieties of marble as any place, because the lower limestones have the greatest uplift there

Quartzite.

On Reed's Creek, some distance from its mouth, not far from the line between the counties of Lee and Van Buren, are heavy beds of quartzite. The color of it is nearly white—sometimes, a light blue; and it is so slightly adhesive that it can easily be shaved off with a spade. Plasterers, when working in the neighborhood, are accustomed to obtain it for their 'finishing-coat.' Those of them who have used this, and also that obtained at the Falls of St. Anthony, say that the two kinds are just alike. Examined with a magnifier, the sandstone on Reed's Creek is sharply angular, and appears to be very pure quartz. The slight coloring it has received has probably been obtained from the superincumbent earth. For plastering purposes, it cements as well with lime as that of the Falls; and if it really be like it, these beds are a source whence can be obtained the best materials for the manufacture of crystal glass.

Clays.

Passing by the kinds from which common brick are made, and those used for earthen and stone-ware, the coal measures abound in 'fire-clay.' Fire-proof bricks are wrought of this for the use of foundries, furnaces, and in all cases and places where there is an exposure to intense heat. In the Eastern States, it has sometimes been necessary to import these bricks from England. The cost of them has been as high as $50 per thousand. It is desirable that fire-places and ovens should be constructed of them; and where fire-clay is plenty, as in the Valley, there is no reason why they should not be. But bricks are heavy articles of transport; and until there are railroad facilities of carriage, that one item of cost will prevent extensive business in this kind of manufacture. With such facilities, there appears no good reason why this clay should not be worked. And as to quantity, the Valley can supply the United States, with Cuba and Mexico annexed!

Iron Ore.

Iron has been found in several places, though no beds are known in the Valley of so rich a character as those of the 'Iron Mountain,' in Missouri. Owen found this ore in Marion County, in beds which he considered would hereafter be worked. Specimens taken from them and examined had a specific gravity of 3·45; that of pure iron being

7·7. By analysis, they contained 35 per cent. of iron. This iron, as to richness and quality, is almost exactly like the 'Cairnhill Black Band,' of Scotland, which is extensively worked. Other and heavier beds have been discovered since Owen's Survey; but whether rich or not, is not certainly known; the ore not having been tested by competent men. In such circumstances, it is not possible to speak of this ore with great definiteness.

Gypsum, or Plaster of Paris.

This is chemically known as the sulphate of lime. The heaviest beds of it in the United States are to be found in the vicinity of Fort Dodge, Webster county. They are from 20 to 30 feet thick, and show themselves on both sides of the river for miles; and they extend back each way an unknown distance. By analysis, this gypsum contains 70·8 per cent. of sulphate of lime.

On one acre, with an average thickness of 20 feet, there will be 871·200 cubic feet; on one square mile, 557,568,000 cubic feet; and on three miles square, 5,018,112,000 cubic feet and 308,031,428 tons.

Before closing this paper on the minerals of the Valley, it is proper to say that the survey of Dr. Owen was made by order of the United States, and had for its more special object the discovery of mineral lands, such as the Government might wish to reserve. The principal minerals sought were lead and copper. The coal-field was surveyed and mapped down, while the other minerals noticed in this paper received only incidental attention and secondary con sideration—some of them, no mention at all.

Collectively, the minerals of this Valley, as now known, are extensive and valuable. They constitute one of the many items which render their locality so attractive. It is traversed by one of the most beautiful rivers on earth; 400 miles in length, a large portion of it 250 yards in breadth: capable of floating steamers a part of the year, and affording water-power to any desirable extent: with a landscape of great and charming variety, groves, and forests, and prairies, in constant alternation, and possessing a soil "scarcely excelled for fertility, perhaps, in the world," why should it not be thronged with inhabitants? It is the centre of the "Mesopotamia of the West," in a more important sense than that of its position. Let but the iron horse traverse the whole length of the Valley, and its silver stream will be skirted with cities and villages in as great continuity as is the Bosphorus; meanwhile, its agricultural, and mineral, and manufactured exports, will amount to many millions of dollars annually.

Col. Mix, of Dubuque, in the summer and fall of 1855, made a thorough exploration of that portion of the route of the Dubuque and Pacific Railroad, extending from the Mississippi to the Missouri River. From his report we extract the following:

NOTE.—The author spent a portion of the past year in making investigations of the location and extent of the beds of coal, lead, gypsum, &c., in Iowa, and has set forth the result of his researches in a work entitled "Parker's Sectional and Geological Map of Iowa." By reference to this map, and to the chapters on particular counties, in this work, it will be seen that discoveries of iron, copper, lead, and coal, have been made in localities not specified in the foregoing paper.

"Attention has been directed to the coal field. Its eastern measure, from geological signs, is first indicated near the corners of Grundy, Hardin, Butler and Franklin Counties, in range 18, and probably extends a few miles beyond the Boyer, in range 39. Croppings-out on the Iowa, Boone and Des Moines Rivers; and the veins are only thus far worked from necessitous demand. They are reported to be from 1 to 8 feet thick; but those that fell under our observation are from 3 to 7 feet. It is believed there are three strata, and the middle the thickest. Its measure in this latitude is broad beyond question, and it may be uncovered on Coon and Cedar Rivers. It is imagined its basin on this line lies below the head waters of Skunk River and the south fork of the Iowa. Small formations are apparent in the Little Sioux and Missouri bluffs, but doubtful if in veins of sufficient thickness for working. In passing through the centre of the State, its discovery was asserted in very many places, but it remains, however, for scientific and practical mining to discover and bring forth for comfort and riches, Nature's too often well concealed and hidden mineral treasures.

"Gypsum, in inexhaustible quantity, abounds at Fort Dodge, on both sides of the Des Moines River, and is unsurpassed in quality between the oceans. It is, from personal examination, of greater extent than Professor Owen's report represents. The idea that constant culture will not impoverish the richest soil is not to be entertained; and the value of this article in agriculture, and for other purposes, is almost incalculable. Coal, iron ore, and building rock, which in fineness and durability the Quincy granite does not excel, are found in this vicinity. Rock of most excellent quality is also seen on the Iowa and Cedar Rivers, particularly at Cedar Falls.

"The specimen of iron ore handed you, is found on Des Moines River, some 12 miles above Fort Dodge. Of its existence on Iowa River, in the immediate vicinity of the best part of the coal formation, there is very little doubt. Whether of compensating per centage for manufacture we could not determine, as the specimens shown were corroded by time.

"At Iowa Falls, on Iowa River, there exists in quantity, a limestone or marble of cream color, and admitting the finest polish. If it has not the beauty of Eastern white or variegated, it surely possesses equal durability and fineness of texture. Other marble is also found on the same river, having an intermixture of a brownish color. This item, too, which is a novelty in the West, will also yield its revenue.

"Coal, providentially so abundant in the heart of the State, will be in almost unlimited demand in Northwestern Illinois, Western Wisconsin, Minnesota, a large portion of our own State, and for the steamboats on both rivers.

"A striking characteristic of this route, and worthy of marked observation, is that every river, with the exception of those two branches heretofore mentioned, flows over either a pebbled, gravelly, or rocky bottom. Their banks, with the exception of Des Moines at Fort Dodge, also stated, are very easy of access and departure, and materials are at hand for cheap bridging."

5*

CHAPTER IX.

POPULATION — IMMENSE IMMIGRATION OF 1855.

The population of the Territory in 1836, was 10,531; in 1840, it was 43,017; in 1850, 192,214. The census, as returned by the Secretary of State, taken in the spring of 1854, is as follows: Males, 170,302; females, 154,900; total population, 325,202. Voters, 59,984; militia, 50,284; aliens, 10,373; colored males, 258; colored females, 222; blind, 27; deaf and dumb, 28; insane, 47; idiots, 7. There is one vote to every five and a half and a fraction of the population.

According to this last census, the number of males exceeds that of the females some 16,000. Let the Yankee girls take the hint when they see these figures.

The number of inhabitants in the State in January, 1855, has been estimated at upwards of 500,000. Those who have seen and can realize that Iowa is the mouth of the great Stream of Humanity, whose tributaries extend far and wide, into every State and many nations — that stream which is daily and hourly pouring into this great, and fertile, and beautiful State, its hundreds and thousands, cannot but predict that in 1860 Iowa will be peopled by more than a million of hardy, energetic, and intelligent inhabitants.

By some, this may be deemed a wild speculation; but we think we have good and sufficient reasons for placing our estimate thus. That the reader may have some idea of the immense influx into Iowa, we will annex a few extracts which appeared in the newspapers at different points in the State last summer and fall.

Of the Immense Immigration of 1854–5.

The *Iowa City Reporter* says:

"Mr. Watts, of this city, has recently returned from a trip East. On his way home, he represents the immigration bound for Iowa as astonishing and unprecedented. For miles and miles, day after day, the prairies of Illinois are lined with cattle and wagons, pushing on towards our prosperous State.

"A point beyond Peoria, Mr. Watts remained over night; where he was informed that, during a single month, *seventeen hundred and forty-three* wagons had passed, and *all for Iowa*. Allowing five persons to a wagon, which is a fair average, we have 8715 souls to add to our population. This being but the immigration of the month, and upon one route only out of many, it would not be an unreasonable assertion to say that 50,000 men, women, and children will have come into this State by the first of December, reckoning from the first of September."

Remembering that those spoken of by Mr. Watts all came by wagons, please add this item, from the *Chicago Press*:

"Most of the passenger trains came in last week with

two locomotives; and the reason of this great increase of power will be understood when it is known that *twelve thousand passengers* arrived from the East, by the Michigan Southern road, during the last week — a city in the short space of six days!"

To the above, add the crowds who ascend the Mississippi and Missouri upon every boat, of whom as many as 600 have passed St. Louis in one day!

The *Oskaloosa Times* says:

"From early morning till night-fall, the covered wagons are passing through the place."

"We learn from old citizens that the tide of immigration is this year greater than they have ever known before."

"We should think at least a thousand persons pass through Oskaloosa every week, about these times, on their way westward."

"Not an hour in the day but we see teams 'hauling up' on the Square."

The *Davenport Commercial* adds:

"That's our case, precisely. Our ferry is busy all hours in passing over the large canvas-backed wagons, densely populated with becoming Iowaians. An army of mechanics have added 300 buildings to this city during the past season, yet every nook and corner of them are engaged before they are finished; but our hospitable citizens will not allow any to suffer for want of a shelter. In several instances the citizens have, like true aborigines, withdrawn to close quarters, and given their parlors to those who have come to make their homes among us and were unable to find dwellings. There is not a vacant dwelling or business room in the city."

The *Burlington Telegraph* says:

"20,000 immigrants have passed through the city within the last thirty days, and they are still crossing at the rate of 600 and 700 a day. We have these facts from the ferry folks, who keep a sort of running register. About one team in a hundred is labelled 'Nebraska;' all the rest are marked 'Iowa.'"

The *Dubuque Tribune* says:

"Daily—yes, hourly—immigrants are arriving in this and neighboring counties from Ohio, Kentucky, Indiana, and Illinois. All are in raptures at the lovely sights which here greet their gaze; and they with one accord yield the palm to Western Iowa for lovely prairies, beautiful groves of timber, and meandering streams of water."

The editor of the *Dubuque Reporter* thus speaks of the "*Prospects of Iowa*":

"Never before, in the history of this northwestern region of the United States, has there been a more gratifying spectacle than that now presented to those who take an interest in its progress and welfare. Viewing the almost countless throng of immigrants that crowd our streets, and learning that a similar scene is visible at every other point along the Mississippi border of Iowa, the spectator is naturally led to infer that a general exodus is taking place in the Eastern States of the Union, as well as in those that, but a few years ago, were denominated the West.

"Day by day the endless procession moves on—a mighty

army of invasion, which, were its objects other than peace, and a holy, fraternal, cordial league with its predecessors, their joint aim to conquer this fair and alluring domain from the wild dominion of nature would strike terror into the boldest hearts. They come by hundreds and thousands from the hills and valleys of New England, bringing with them that same untiring, indomitable energy and perseverance, that have made their native States the admiration of the world, and whose influence is felt wherever enterprise has a votary or commerce spreads a sail; with intellects sharpened to the keenest edge, and brawny arms to execute the firm resolves of their iron will, and gathering fresh accessions, as they sweep across the intermediate country, from the no less thrifty and hardy population of New York, Ohio, and Indiana. Tarrying no longer amongst us than is necessary for them to select their future home, away they hie to the capacious and inviting plains, that spread themselves interminably, ready to yield, almost without preparation, their rich latent treasures.

"Soon will be seen innumerable the farmer's comfortable abode, and the frequent thriving village, with its 'people's college,' as its highest worldly pride, and close at hand the house of God, with spire pointing to heaven, as if to remind the worshippers of the source to which they are indebted for all the store of blessings they enjoy. And soon, too, in the wake of such a mighty rush and all its soul-swelling consequences, will follow the laying out and construction of those great works that will link us to the wide-spread members of our confederacy, over which the iron horse, more terrible in the fierceness of his strength than the war-steed of Job, will snort his triumphant ha, ha! as he bounds along in his tireless race. Science, in turn, will rear her loftiest fanes, and plant deep in the hearts of her disciples the seeds of a deathless devotion to the institutions of our common country.

"And to what, let us ask, is the high tide setting into Iowa fairly to be ascribed?

"We take it on ourselves to answer that the unanimous consent of those who have investigated her claims accords her a climate of unequalled salubrity, a soil of the most generous fertility, and a geographical position unsurpassed by that of any other Western State; in a word, that naturally she contains within her limits all the elements which, properly availed of by man, will secure his highest temporal prosperity and happiness. During the past year, she has been peculiarly favored. Whilst the contiguous States, and many of those more remote, have yielded harvests diminished by drought in the ratio of from a fourth to a half, hers has been at least equal to an average one. She is thus able to supply not only her producers, but likewise all who have since come, and are yet to arrive this year. This has been of incalculable advantage to her. Inasmuch as every immigrant comes provided with the means for entering land and defraying expenses till he can make a crop, money has been in freer circulation here than in any other part of the country. A fact equally gratifying is, that the immigration hither numbers in its ranks many men of wealth, who consequently bring to us an accession of capital that must of course produce results which are usually unseen in new states for years after their settlement.

"We conclude our remarks on the prospects of Iowa by tendering our congratulations to her citizens on the proud and enviable position she occupies — a position obtained without effort, and which is but a foretaste of that she will attain as her strength is increased and her concentrated energies directed to the securing of a yet loftier elevation."

The editor of the *Keokuk Whig* thus speaks, under the announcement of

"'STILL THEY COME!' By railways and steamers, the flood of immigration continues pouring into the great West. The lake-shore roads are crowded to their utmost capacity; single trains of fourteen or fifteen cars, all full of men, women, and a large sprinkling of children, are almost daily arriving at Chicago. The Ohio River steamers are crowded in the same way. On Friday last, two steamers brought into St. Louis some 600 passengers; most of whom, being destined for the northwest, have already passed through this place. And 'still they come,' from Pennsylvania, from Ohio, Indiana, and other States, until, by the side of this exodus, that of the Israelites becomes an insignificant item, and the greater migrations of later times are scarcely to be mentioned. Whether the older States are suffering by this rapid depletion, or how long they can endure it, is their own look-out. Certain it is that Iowa in particular, and the other Western and Northwestern States generally are rapidly filling up with a hardy, industrious and wealth-producing population. Let them come! Here is room, and to spare! Here is a theatre for human operations on the grandest scale! Here is the place for the young man, just starting out in life, for the old man, seeking to provide for his children, for 'all sorts of men,' in search of fortune, fame, or wealth; for any one, also, who has an eye and a soul for Nature in her grandest forms of lavish profusion and splendid magnificence.

"There is something in the 'growing, glowing West,' with her limitless prairies, her mighty rivers, her mountains of iron, the lavish richness of her all-bountiful soil, that expands the soul of man, and elevates him above the narrow, cramped, and confined ideas of those who are accustomed only to the well-worn channels and small conventionalities of older hum-drum communities. There the 'new man' is apt to find himself an unwelcome jostler, his intrusion viewed askance, his elbow-room begrudged him, and his presence tolerated only upon condition of his accepting the procrustean standard of hoary and respectable 'use and wont;' unless, indeed, a position can be asserted and maintained by force of very superior talent, or unusual accidental advantages. But here all is new, and plastic, and vigorous. Men are wanted here, and are welcomed. And here at once is found a boundless and untrammelled field of enterprise, adequate to the elastic energies of ingenious youth or mature manhood. It is curious to watch the development of a comer from the old-fogy settlements: to see his mind expand, his eye light up with the fire of a renewed energy, and his whole nature grow to the liberal standard of Nature's doings in the West.

"Therefore, we repeat again, let them come — old and young, men and women, boys and girls, with or without 'plunder.' Let them flee from their tax-ridden and miserably governed Egypts in Ohio and Pennsylvania, to the Land of Promise, flowing with something better than milk and honey, and possessing capabilities such as they have hardly dreamed of. Here they shall find welcome homes; and, while they speedily help themselves to attain better fortunes, they shall also have a hand in the proud labor of building up the mighty Empire of the Mississippi Valley."

The editor of the *Keokuk Dispatch*, after returning from a two-weeks' furlough, says:

"No one can travel up and down the Mississippi without being astonished at the immigration constantly pouring into Iowa from all parts of the country; but especially from Indiana and Ohio.

"Two gentlemen from Richmond County, Ohio, told us that from that County alone 1000 persons were coming to Iowa this fall; at every ferry on the river crowds are waiting to cross; and the land-offices all over the State are unable to meet the demands upon them by those who are eager to enter lands.

"Our journey led us into Jackson and Jones Counties, where we met, in all directions, indications of rapid settlement, thrift, and energy. We spent some days in Jones County, on the prairie watered by Mineral Creek, and learned that but a year ago there were forty thousand acres of unentered land, while there is not now as much as amounts to a section to be had. Although the prairie is but a few miles in extent, there are already forty habitations upon it.

"When we take into account the central position of Iowa in our confederacy, and the fact of the rapid development of her resources, we can easily believe that she is destined to become, at no distant day, all that the most sanguine hope for. Her salubrious climate, the abundance of water, and the favorable distribution of timber, all contribute to give Iowa pre-eminence among the Western States in the minds of those who are exchanging a residence in the East for one in the West."

OF THE IMMIGRATION IN 1855.

The *Rock Islander* thus speaks of the tide of immigration flowing into Iowa, at Davenport:

"'Westward the star of Empire takes its way,' sang good old Bishop Berkeley, a hundred years ago. Whoever wants a practical illustration of what is now a fact, but was then a prophesy, need only watch our ferry a single hour. Hundreds of muslin-covered wagons, bearing wives and children, and household goods, and driven by stalwart men, seeking a new home in the mighty West, cross the Mississippi at this point weekly. It is a tide which knows no ebb, but still keeps flowing, ever flowing, onward toward the rich prairies of Nebraska and the setting sun."

An Ohio paper thus speaks:

"The last wonder at the eastward is the immense immigration westward. Nothing like it here or there was ever before known. It is estimated, from the way it has commenced, that it will exceed that of any previous year full fifty per cent. Many circumstances have conspired to produce this movement, but the hard times for the past year eastward, and the abundance of good and cheap land westward, with the ambition of the masses to better their condition in life, are the stimulating causes."

The *Washington County*, Iowa, paper says:

"Our town is daily full of strangers from the Eastern States; seeking homes amongst us, and purchasing property both in town and country. Every house and every room in the town is filled to its utmost capacity, and yet the demand is not supplied. The mail coaches from every direction are crowded with passengers, piled in, shaken down, and running over; and besides this kind of conveyance, private passenger hacks 'loaded down to the guards,' are seen on the streets and at the hotels almost hourly.

"With the present rate of emigration, Iowa must ere long become one of the most populous States in the north-western portion of the Union."

The *Chicago Press* thus speaks of the Western movement:

"We have heretofore referred to the fact, that the amount of travel West was much larger than the Eastern movement. This is true now, and will be till the vast fertile country West and North-west of us becomes generally settled, and its resources fully developed. In the older States the young and enterprising are seeking a home in the great central valley of the continent, and for many years to come the population of the New England and Middle States must increase very slowly, and in some of them, perhaps, not at all; while that in most of the central States will be told in millions.

"We learn from William M. Larabee, Esq., secretary of the Galena and Chicago Union Railroad, that during the past year, the passengers on that road going West have numbered about forty thousand more than those coming East. This fact is very significant, and indicates that over this thoroughfare alone more than three thousand passengers per month have gone West, and made their homes in the rich lands lying towards the setting sun."

The *Chicago Journal* of May 3, says:

"WESTWARD.—Last night the city was invaded, and hundreds had not where to lay their heads. The hotels were compelled to turn all who came in the evening trains away, being unable to accommodate them."

The *Burlington Pantagraph* of a recent date, says:

"The van of the great emigrant army has been passing through our town for the last two or three weeks. The average through this place for some time past has been about fifty wagons daily, generally followed by droves of fine looking cattle, and attended by all the other indications of thrift and enterprise; and wherever they may choose to pitch their tent there will be planted the elements of an intelligent and prosperous community.

We could occupy pages more in giving like extracts from the press in various parts of the State; but the foregoing will suffice.

CHAPTER X.

GENERAL REMARKS.

Immigration—Rivers and Lakes—Mineral Resources—Onward March of Civilization.

It is truly gratifying to witness the rapidity with which our noble State is increasing in population. Tens of thousands of hardy, industrious "sons of the soil," with their families and herds, are lining every thoroughfare into the State, attracted by our beautiful scenery, rich soil, salubrious climate, and superior natural advantages. To this class we extend a hand of welcome—for them we have "a home for all." To non-resident speculators in lands, who enter them to hold, unimproved, for high prices, we extend no invitation; believing them a disadvantage to the State, and an interposing obstacle between us and prosperity.

Aware of the difficulty the immigrant from the Eastern States labors under in obtaining a correct knowledge of the West—of its vast resources, its immense fields for cultivation, spread out in untold beauty, inviting the husbandman to partake of the bounty which a beneficent Being has spread out before him, I hope to furnish my readers with some facts that will prove interesting and profitable to those intending to make their homes in Iowa. I would speak of our beautiful rivers, productive soil, and healthful climate;

of the glassy lakes, whose pebbled shores have for ages been the haunts of the elk, the buffalo, and the deer, and whose waters abound in the finest specimens of the finny tribe. These solitary places, that have slept in beauty so long, have been awakened into life. The woodman's axe now begins to echo on the banks of our streams, and the hum of voices resounds upon our lakes. Civilization, in her westward march, has aroused the deer from his lair; and where, but yesterday, the wolf held undisputed sway, the familiar bark of the farmer's faithful dog is heard.

Probably no State in the Union has ever been settled with greater rapidity, or in so short a period of time gained greater renown, than Iowa.

Bounded on the east by that noblest of rivers, the Mississippi, and on the west by the Missouri, cut up and intersected at the most important points by railroads, projected and under contract, possessing almost inexhaustible supplies of lead in the north, and of coal in the south, of lime, sand, and other building-stone in almost every portion of the State, she combines within her borders, resources that must render her, in point of position and wealth, one of the most important States in the Republic.

The Climate of Iowa may be compared with that of New Jersey and the vicinity of New York City; except that we have not here as much rain and foggy weather as they have. Here it is, in general, an unbroken winter from the middle of November till January; when we are invariably visited with the *January thaw;* after which, the weather is generally mild, and gradually merges into spring. We have but little snow — seldom sufficient for sleighing, and but few sleds or sleighs are manufactured. We are free from the sudden changes so common to New England; the weather is less variable. Our storms are from the east, our showers from the west.

Cultivation and yield of Wheat, Corn, Oats, Potatoes and Onions.

Our wheat is sown in March, and our corn planted the last of April and first of May. But little winter wheat is grown here; the light snows are insufficient to protect it from winter-killing. Spring wheat is raised in great abundance, and of a good quality. Corn is raised in large quantities; and all the products of the earth, congenial to this climate grow, with but little labor. Seldom is the hoe used in the corn or potatoe-field — the horse and plough do the work in general. Of the wheat crop, 40 bushels to the acre is considered a good crop; and of corn, 50, 60, and 75 bushels are raised to the acre; 400 and 500 bushels of potatoes and onions are common to the acre. I know of large crops being taken from the ground — such as 100 bushels of oats to the acre, and the same of corn; but they are not common, and such tales only serve to heighten the fancy of those who intend immigrating, and mislead them.

The Soil and Prospects of the Farmer East and West compared.

A man cannot come here and grow rich in idleness: he must work. Our soil is prolific, but must have care and culture. It is true that man can live with less labor than in the older States; the soil is easier tilled. He can make himself a home much sooner, and far more easily, than those who purchase land in northern New York, Ohio, and Indiana. How many are there in those States who have toiled for years to cut away the timber and burn it; expending, on an average, $10 or $12 an acre before the plow can enter the land, and then be used with great difficulty among the stumps, roots, and rocks; and how many farmers are there now, in those States, going down to the grave in the meridian of life with a worn-out and broken constitution! Compare the new settlement of those States with a settlement in Iowa. Here, the immigrant enters upon his land, perhaps, at government price — $1·25 per acre; or, if he pays $5, or even $10, per acre, he finds it free from all obstacles in making a farm. For the sum of $2·50, the prairie is broken up, and often corn is planted the first year, by striking the axe into the turf and dropping the corn, which yields 15 to 25 bushels per acre. This is called sod-corn. The second year, the turf is rotten, the ground easily tilled, and the husbandman's labors are crowned with success.

Enclosing Farms — Osage Orange as a Substitute for Board, Wire, or Sod Fences.

To enclose the land, various kinds of fencing have been tried. Among the early settlers, the sod fence was made by those who had a scarcity of timber, but proved a perfect failure. The soil being too alluvial and loamy to sustain itself, the common board fence was resorted to, till, more recently, the wire fence has been introduced, and succeeds well where it is properly made. In most parts of the State, hogs are not allowed to run at large, and of course less fencing is required. It is now sufficiently demonstrated, by trial of a few, that the Osage-orange hedge is to be the great remedy for lack of timber upon our prairies: it has been tested, and found that a hedge of this shrub will turn any kind of animal, from a horse to a sucking pig, in three or four years. This fence can be made for forty cents per rod, and warranted, or no pay. Upon the prairie, where there is not much range of cattle, the hedge can be planted and grown without fence to protect it; nothing will eat the plant, and the few that might be destroyed by being trod upon, can easily be replaced. In fencing, then, 100 acres square, the expense would be $250, for a fence that would last for ever. It will need training only, as it does not sprout from the roots. But, half of this fence will be for the accommodation of your neighbor; consequently, your cost will be but half this sum. In order to make this fence, the ground must be broken some eight or ten feet wide, upon the line of fence, one year before the planting of the hedge. I understand that a contract has been made recently, by the Illinois Central Railroad, to fence the entire road, some 300 miles, with the Osage orange.

For immediate use, those who have no timber must fence with lumber; which is $15 per thousand feet; and the white-cedar post can be had for $10 per hundred. It will take 1280 posts, eight feet apart, to fence 100 acres with wire or boards; the amount of either of the latter will be regulated according to the number of strands; which may be three or five. There is but one great deficiency in our State — the scarcity of timber. But we hope for a substitute in the Osage orange, as far as fencing is concerned.

Renting, building, Brick-making — No Vacant Lands near the Mississippi River.

Tillable land is now rented at $1·75 to $2·00 per acre. The first tenement of the settler is generally of small dimensions; reared in haste, and ultimately to form the kitchen part of his future dwelling. Brick is made in all parts of the State; and in most parts, the limestone rock is abundant, and often used for entire dwellings for man and beast. The vacant land or lands, still owned by the Government, have now become very scarce in the settled portions of the State. No selections of good land can now be made within fifty or seventy-five miles of the Mississippi River. The immense immigration of the last two years has secured all choice lands in the vicinity of settlements and railroads; and the only chance of the immigrant for land at $1·25 per acre, is to go back into the interior of the State. Many prefer purchasing nearer market—nearer the Mississippi River; where unimproved land can be had at from $9 to $20 per acre, and improved farms at from $20 to $40, and even $50 per acre—according to the value of improvements.

Iowa as it is, and as the Immigrant may expect to find it—Earnest Labor the Price of Success.

The immigrant must not come here as many do—expecting to find first rate land, with timber and water, all spread out before him, very near some city or town, for $1·25 per acre; it is not to be had. Nor must he come expecting to find Iowa a desolate, dreary, uncultivated waste, with here and there a green spot, inhabited by pioneers living in log cabins and just merging into civilization; neither must he come expecting to live at ease, enjoying the luxuries of life and health, rolling in upon him without any exertion. A home can be had by the poorest, with prudence and economy. *No place in the wide world can offer greater inducements to the immigrant than Iowa; but he must look at it as it is.* No fancied sketch must weave around his imagination sudden wealth or unreal beauties, seen only in the dreary picture before him. He may fancy Iowa a garden, and, roaming over its prairies, gather flowers from its rich soil, and exclaim with the Indian, in ecstasies of delight, 'I-o-wah!'—'I have found the beautiful land!' but it will never make him rich, nor create for him a happy home, without toil and labor.

Unentered Lands—Immense Immigration of 1855—*Central Iowa—Best Portions of the State yet Unsettled—The Destiny of Iowa.*

There are yet large bodies of land subject to entry at the government price—$1·25 per acre. Early last season, there was much upon the line of the various projected railroads subject to sale; there are none at this time within less than ten miles of the railroad. The timber-lands of this section of country are all secured; nothing remains but prairie. The woodlands must be purchased at second rates, from $8 to $15 per acre. These back counties, even to Council Bluffs, are better timbered than those within fifty miles of the Mississippi River, except in the northern part of Iowa. Along the upper Des Moines and Boon rivers are heavily timbered lands at reasonable prices. The vacant lands of Iowa are being entered rapidly, and those who would get good locations at government price must attend to the matter without delay. The immense immigration to the interior of Iowa this season exceeds, by far, all former years. The roads are full of immigrant teams; the groves, creeks, and woodlands seem alive with men, women, and children encamped in wagons, tents, and cabins, until houses can be erected.

There are nearly one hundred counties of land in this State surveyed and in market; two-thirds of that number are organized, and contain a population of from 500 to 25,000 each: the river tier of counties being the first settled and most densely populated. Central Iowa is the best body of land in the State; and, in all probability, the State of Iowa is the best in the United States. The better portions of Iowa are not settled yet. The immigrant must not think that Iowa is all sold, or in the hands of speculators. Go where you may, westward or northward, and the boundless prairie is spread out before you, dotted here and there with its groves and its gentle rivers, skirted with timber; and you find no diminution in beauty or richness of soil: the same deep, black loam is found northward to the St. Peter's River, and westward to the Missouri. The immigrant who is willing to penetrate unsettled portions, and endure the privations incident to a frontier life, can lay, for himself and his children, the foundations of a fortune and a home that will make glad the hearts of his children's children; for Iowa is destined to be the most densely populated State in the Union.

How often has the thought passed through my mind, while rambling over these fertile plains, of the thousands of human beings whose lot has been cast in more sterile lands, bound down by oppression and servitude! What happiness could be offered to the starving millions of the Old World, could the ill-gotten treasures of tyrants be converted to their use, and the uncultivated wastes, that now are only kept for the use of a few wandering tribes of Indians, were made the abodes of civilized men! The onward progress of the Anglo-Saxon race will soon open these vast resources for the benefit of man; and I believe that many of us now upon the stage of action, will see these fertile vales teeming with their ten thousand flocks, and hear from the happy cottages the general anthem of thanksgiving and praise, amid these beautiful glens ana dales, until the prolonged note shall sigh upon the Rocky Mountain's top, and the echo be heard along the Shores of the Pacific Ocean.

CHAPTER XI.

INSTRUCTIONS TO THE NEW-COMER RESPECTING THE SELECTION, ENTRY, OR PURCHASE AND CULTIVATION OF PRAIRIE LANDS.

THE purchaser from Government, if he be a stranger in the country, must first go to the Land-office of the District in which lie the lands that he intends to enter. There are in Iowa nine Land-offices, each of which represents several counties. At either of these the immigrant will be furnished with small township maps, showing all the vacant or unentered lands, up to the date of application. With these he repairs to the spot; but, without the aid of a surveyor, or some person who understands the mode of government surveys, he will be totally unprepared to make selections, as the "metes and bounds" upon the prairie, or marked trees of the forest, will be all *Greek* to him. He may gaze upon the goodly land, but for him to *know* what township, range, or section, or any parts thereof, he is on, will be found impossible. He cannot transcribe the hieroglyphics before him. The numbers must be carefully noted by one who *knows*, and who will accompany the immigrant to the Land-office; there he makes his application to the Register, receives a certificate of application, and then presents the same to the Receiver; pays in specie, or with his warrant, or Virginia land-script, and receives a duplicate receipt as having paid for such a tract of land, and, in the course of one or two years, he presents his receipt to the same office, and receives a patent from government; his duplicate receipt. however, is a sufficient warrantee for him to sell and convey the land, and is valid in law.

To enter upon and settle these lands, is the next thing for the immigrant. He first erects a small cabin of boards, or perhaps of logs, sufficient to shield himself and family from "the pitiless peltings of the storm," and, with eyes often beaming with gladness, enters with great alacrity upon the thousand and one little works of necessity and mercy for the comfort and security of man and beast; while the enormous prairie plow is set in motion by one whose business it is to "*break prairie*" at $2·25 per acre. This large machine is, to the new-comer, a curiosity: it is, in all respects, like other plows, but much larger in size; being 10 feet long, and cutting a furrow of some 22 to 24 inches in width. The fore-end of the beam rests upon an axle, with wheels, one of which runs in the furrow and guages the width, acting like the wheel of the locomotive upon the rail. A lever is attached to the fore-end of the beam, running back to the handles, which regulates the depth of furrow, and throws the plow out when desired. When the plow is once set in, it needs no further attention in good prairie, as it runs alone, and the driver has only to attend to his team, which consists of some five yoke of oxen. The roots of the wild grass are much longer and harder to break than the tame. It is considered best to break the ground as shallow as possible, or only to cut a sufficient depth to turn over the *roots of grass;* the soil under it being very loose, and the thinner the sod, the sooner it will rot. Often the farmer sends his boys to drop corn along every third or fourth furrow; and corn is thus produced, with no further care, yielding 30 bushels to the acre. The next season the sod is well rotted, and the ground in prime order for wheat. In the meantime, the immigrant encloses his fields, either with sawed lumber or rails, as circumstances will permit, erects his dwelling, and begins his

"Life on the prairie green,
A home on the boundless waste!"

The soil is ready to till, and but few weeds grow for the first two or three years. As I have before said, corn is planted and grown without using the hoe: the horse and plow do the cultivating.

The Realities of a Pioneer Life — Obstacles to be Surmounted — The Reward in Store.

These are but faint outlines of opening a farm in the West. The immigrant will find trials and hardships spring up around, unlooked for in the old settlement. He will find that his ability to labor is not as great in his new, unacclimated home, as where he came from: the scarcity of labor, the distance from towns, villages, and market, will throw obstacles in the way of his progress, and he may very naturally expect, in a change of climate, sickness in his family; and "the ills that life is heir to," will, perhaps, tread closely upon his heels, and often make him sigh for "*the leeks and the garlics*" he left behind him. There is no fancy work in a frontier life, except to him who is weaned from the world at an early age, and assumes the life of a savage. It may do for the intelligent and enterprising of our eastern cities to build for themselves fancied cottages upon our western lands while they are gorged with the pleasures of a city life; but the *stern reality* of a frontier life will not be all sunshine and happiness; there is labor to be done to enjoy it; there is care and toil, privations and sufferings, universally attendant upon any one's settlement in the new portions of the West; and he who leaves the luxuries of the East and moves to the West, expecting to realize the fancied sketches of *rural felicity*, will be most sadly disappointed. But let him surmount these obstacles, and he can make himself a home that will yield him a rich and lasting harvest.

CHAPTER XII.

SKETCHES BY TRAVELLING CONTRIBUTORS TO THE PRESS, DESCRIPTIVE OF IOWA.

THE following interesting and truthful statistical article from the *Franklin Democrat*, published at Brookville, Ind., was written in reply to a paragraph that appeared in the *American*, a newspaper published in the same town, which spoke disparagingly of Iowa. Mr. Clarkson, the writer, has for twenty years been conductor of a newspaper, and quite recently made a tour through our State, examining its resources and its adaptation to a farming community. He therefore speaks from personal knowledge.

"*Will the Iowa fever abate?*—There is such a rush for Iowa lands, and such a tide of emigration in that direction, that croakers begin to proclaim that 'the Iowa fever is about over.' As sensible men, we ought to look at this subject, if there is to be a revulsion in matters in that region, it is cruel for *wise heads* to permit the *simple* minded populace to rush into danger unwarned. It will not do for prophets to sneeringly say, 'Am I my brother's keeper?'

"But what is taking the people to Iowa? This is a serious question, and should be looked full in the face by every man before he sells his farm and drags his family to a new and unknown country. It is not a sufficient excuse that you were carried away by the popular furor. But the matter is of sufficient importance to demand the closest scrutiny. Will you do so, or will you risk the consequences, and then when you have squandered your means, and beggared your family, regret your rash step.

"We therefore propose to look to this question, and if we err in any matter, for the sake of the interests of crowding thousands, we ask to be corrected.

"Iowa is larger than any other State of the Union, being about 14,000 square miles larger than New York. It has more rich agricultural lands than any other State in the Union. In this matter we speak not at random. There is in Iowa 40,000,000 of acres—two-thirds of which at least is equal to any other lands, in any State, already cleared, and ready for cultivation. Or in other words there are in Iowa about 28,000,000 of acres of rich prairie, requiring no tedious labor to convert it into productive farms. This is more land for real cultivation than there is, or ever will, or can be cultivated in New York and the six New England States. And when cultivated it will produce double the amount to the acre on an average of the products of Northern farms, and with half the labor per acre. And although there is a large portion of Illinois equal in fertility and productiveness to Iowa, yet the south half of Illinois will not compare with it—in fact a large portion is useless. So we can safely say that Iowa in a few years will have more good improved farm lands than the three States of Ohio, Indiana, and Illinois. We dare any one that doubts this, to test it by the figures. By the census of 1850, we learn that Ohio had 9,851,493 acres of improved land, Indiana 5,046,543, and Illinois 5,039,545, in all 19,937,581 acres. When Ohio, Indiana, and Illinois shall add 50 per cent to their farms, they will fall short of the amount which will, without the least contingency or doubt, be cultivated in Iowa in a few years. This is allowing for 12,000,000 of acres in that State for waste and timber, and for wasting with towns and cities. This then is the extent of the field for agricultural operations. Is it not large enough to command our respect?

"It is healthy. This we have spoken of in a previous

article. But it is useless to dwell on this subject. All the land on the face of the earth north of 41 degrees is healthy, unless there be some immediate local cause for disease.

"Its natural commercial advantages are not inferior to any inland State. Its eastern and western borders are swept for the whole extent by the mightiest rivers in the world, the Mississippi and Missouri. It has also the Des Moines, the Iowa, and the Cedar rivers, all navigable for some distance in wet seasons.

And in the construction of its artificial channels of trade there is likely to be more sense manifested than in most States. The railroads projected, and now being vigorously prosecuted, are all running parallel with each other, and far enough apart not to conflict with each other's interests, but so as to accommodate all the citizens of the State. They all run from east to west from the Mississippi to the Missouri. In no other State has nature so positively directed where the great thoroughfares should be made—and nowhere has man been evidently so willing to listen to the teachings of Providence. The roads all run in about equidistant parallel lines through the State. There are four of them now so far advanced, that no one asks 'Will they ever be built?'

"Iowa is finely watered. The water from springs and wells is fine, cool, and healthy. No difficulty in this respect in any part of the State.

"Stone coal is abundant. This in a prairie country is almost indispensable. With it no one is in doubt about what will be done for wood. In fact, without it the country would not be very densely populated, as all its timber is needed for fences and buildings.

"In most parts of the State, building-stone is plenty, and in some places of a superior quality—both limestone and sandstone. This is an item that cannot be overlooked. Portions of Indiana and Illinois are so destitute of building material, as to depreciate the value of their rich lands.

"Then it has the soil—water—coal—stone—rivers, and railroads, to make it a great agricultural State.

"C. F. CLARKSON."

A writer in the *Express and Herald*, Dubuque, makes the following remarks:

"We have traversed the State of Iowa from east to west, from north to south. We have gazed in admiration on her wide and lovely prairies, stretching away on every side as far as the eye could reach, and presenting the appearance of a boundless ocean covered with luxuriant grass. In other sections of the State, we have lingered by her purling streams, as they meandered through her primeval forests. We have stood by the cascades and rapids of her rivers, and know that she possesses water-power sufficient to turn machinery that could supply manufactures for the whole North American Continent. We have also inspected her rich, loamy soil, of almost inexhaustible fertility, and wandered among her thousand rolling lawns and romantic dells, that abound with minerals more valuable than gold.

"The climate is salubrious; the soil exceedingly rich, producing in abundance all the necessaries of life; the water is of unsurpassed quality, and no other known region excels her in virgin springs and bubbling fountains of the most delicious coolness and purity.

"With regard to an advantageous geographical position, Iowa could hardly be rivalled. Her territory lies between two of the largest rivers on the globe, both navigable for many hundreds of miles above her, and making, on the other hand, an open highway of commerce to the ocean within the tropics. Situated as she is, away in the heart of the continent, far from the national frontier, she will never be subject to the inroads of a foreign enemy's troops, in case of war. Such a foe can never penetrate the country so far as to reach her territory.

"To those who never travelled through the West, much that is reported of it is utterly incredible; although western resources, and western capabilities have never been fully described. The State of Iowa alone is capable of sustaining twenty millions of inhabitants, and then will not be so thickly peopled as some European countries. Her whole area is susceptible of cultivation, and were its powers fully developed, we have no hesitancy in saying that it would produce sufficient food to sustain fifty millions of people.

"In relation to the climate, the soil, the water-power, and the capabilities of Iowa, there is one thing we would say, namely, if any one has doubts about them let him *come* and *see*. Travelling facilities are good, and if you do not like our beautiful State, it is easy to get away."

The following true and eloquent remarks are from a letter to the *New York Tribune*, descriptive of the Upper Mississippi; written by Charles A. Dana, Esq., one of its editors:

"Certainly, of all our rivers, the Mississippi is the most picturesque, and most beautiful. I speak now of that portion of it above the mouth of the Missouri; for the rest I have not seen. Magnitude with the most delicate finish, grandeur of outline with exquisite beauty of detail, are the characteristics of its scenery. The broad and powerful stream is broken by frequent islands covered with dense foliage, which, at this season at least, is deliciously fresh and green, and bordered by lofty bluffs, far more beautiful than the Palisades of the Hudson, rising in every fantastic variety of form, with abrupt and craggy rocks in front, but with the most perfect green sward stretching back to the prairie in the rear, or sloping down in lonely hollows and charming nooks that break the continuity of this river wall, and give constant change and delight to the bachelor. These hills all wear the aspect of old cultivation; and the groves of oak that dot their smooth surface, scattered along their sides, or perched like orchards on their summits, have nothing wild, and favor the illusion. The rocks that form the foundation of the bluffs, and chiefly face the river, do not rise abruptly from the water's edge, but break out about half way up the height, to tower perpendicularly and broken, in the form of ancient walls, or castle battlements; so that the very Rhine does not seem more historic in its appearance. At a little distance, so regular are these walls, so true often the culminating point, so regular the abrasures of time and weather, that it is difficult not to believe that some race of barbarians built these fastnesses, and long ago left them to fall to ruin. As I said, no river is so rich in all the elements of beauty—and there are Indian legends enough for romantic association—but, above all, no river is so rich in all the elements of power. We gaze with wonder at these astonishing fields, prepared by nature herself, where the first tool of the pioneer is the plow—and at this soil, whose teeming richness and facility of culture announces the future home of millions. There's no region on earth, I think, which can sustain a larger population than that on both sides of the Northern Mississippi. A rich soil, suited to every product of the temperate zone, and absolutely inviting the hand of the farmer; a climate genial but not enervating; frequent streams to afford water-power, and fuel abundant on the earth; the great river for a highway, and railroads, which in forty-eight hours land the traveller on the Atlantic—with all these advantages the entire country must become the home of one of the freest, most intelligent, most powerful, and most independent communities of the world. Nowhere else has the hand of Providence so marked out the foundations of an empire; nowhere else is there such an influx of immigration from all directions."

The following is extracted from the contributions to the *Lutheran Observer*, by a clergyman, travelling in Iowa:

"We now come to Iowa, which is like the valley of

Eshcol, or the land of Goshen. The first impression has a powerful effect for good or evil. A man entering into Iowa at this point, is very favorably impressed—you have now passed over the railroad for more than 1000 miles, and you have passed through forests and prairies in Ohio, Indiana, Michigan and Illinois, and you are almost ready to imagine that you have passed beyond the boundaries of civilization; or at most you look for nothing more than the effects produced by the spray of the waves of civilization as they roll into the west. But you are mistaken; you land at Dubuque, Davenport, Burlington, Keokuk, or Muscatine, and find yourself in the very heart of civilization and refinement. You see magnificent churches, and gorgeous dwellings, and large, wide streets. Everything has an air of neatness and purity. And then too you see indications of life and animation—you see the large stores and warehouses groaning under the weight of their valuable commodities—you hear the puffing of the steam-engine, and hear the cheerful ringing of the anvil. You can hardly think it possible that you are more than 1000 miles west of Philadelphia, and in a land where the savage, but a few years since, was sole occupant. But so it is. You look round awhile in the city, and then you ascend the rising ground back of the city to take your first view of Iowa, for up to this time you have seen nothing of this beautiful State, but a little slip of land between the river and the bluff. The bluff is covered with forest trees, and you have to pass on nearly a mile before you have a fair view of Iowa, but when you get out of the forest, a view bursts in upon your vision, such as you have never seen before, unless you saw it in some other part of Iowa. Language utterly fails to describe such a panoramic view. Oh, it is a glorious sight! It would be worth a journey from the Atlantic, just to gaze upon it for one half hour, and then return and see it no more. The view that bursts in upon you is not an Alpine one, to strike you dumb with amazement and terror, nor is it the long-stretching, low, flat, and uninteresting view of a Texan or Illinois prairie, that reminds you of the smooth and unruffled lake. But you have a panorama of a soft, green, and gently undulating world of beauty and loveliness, stretching out into the blue distance, bounded by the gently curving heavens, and dotted all over with the habitations of man, and beautifully variegated with flowers and trees. Many have crossed wide oceans to see sights and wonders, and never saw one like this. You have before you a panoramic view of from eight to twelve hundred square miles of as fine and undulating, and fertile prairie as is to be found in the world. It looks like a land of enchantment where the fairies might reside. It is the vale of Tempe, on a huge and colossal scale. The far distant horizon seems fringed with trees, whose green foliage looks like festoons. This beautiful country is dotted all over with neat farm-houses, and variegated with orchards and groves planted by the hands of man. There are no stones, and although much undulating, or rather rolling, yet it is nowhere so abrupt as to be even inconvenient for the plow. The fertility of the soil is very great, so much so, that if you but tickle the earth, even with a wooden implement, an abundant crop will smile forth. No country in the world will reward the husbandman more abundantly, The farmer has but little to do. When he has his house and stabling built, and his land fenced and broken up, he has but little else to do but gather in his produce, and spend the balance of his life in comfort and ease. Here the man with a little means can enjoy Virgil's "*Otium cum dignitate*," to his heart's content. Timber is scarce, but as coal is abundant, and lumber for building and fencing can always be had at the river, the want of timber is no great loss. Indeed I do not know that it is any great advantage to the farmer to own timber land. In an economical point of view, the farmer can make more by cultivating his prairie land, than he could from his timber. All kinds of fruit trees and grain are easily raised. The water is good. The air is pure and salubrious. The winds are pretty strong—the winters, it is said, are severe, but generally dry, and bracing to the system. Autumnal fevers in some parts of Iowa are common, and will be until the country is more improved, when the malaria which now rises out of the virgin soil will no longer exist. This is the country for our industrious Pennsylvania farmer. Here he can farm without much labor, and by economy add farm to farm. The poor man too can find a home here, and plenty to do and plenty to eat. This is a land like Canaan described in Deuteronomy, viii: 8–9. 'A land of wheat, and barley, and vines—a land wherein thou shalt eat bread without scarceness, thou shalt not lack any thing in it. When thou hast eaten and art full, then thou shalt bless the Lord thy God, for the good land he hath given unto thee.'"

CHAPTER XIII.

RAILROADS.

THERE are several very important railroad lines projected, some of which are partly under contract, and others of which may not be built for years. Three different lines have been explored and surveyed, commencing at Davenport, as follows:

One from Davenport, through Muscatine, thence through the northern part of Louisa County, and through Washington, Keokuk, Mahaska, Marion, Warren, Madison, Adair, Adams, and Montgomery Counties, to the Missouri River, near the mouth of the Platte.

Another from Davenport, through Scott, Johnson, Iowa, Poweshiek, Jasper, Polk, Dallas, Guthrie, Audubon, and Shelby Counties, to the Missouri River, in Pottawattamie County. This was completed to Iowa City, Jan. 1, 1856.

A third line, from Muscatine, through Cedar and Linn Counties, to Cedar Rapids, with a view to the further continuation of the line northwestwardly, into the Territory of Minnesota.

These explorations were made under the direction of Henry Farnam, Chief Engineer; and in December, 1852, an association was formed, under the general laws of Iowa.

The routes embraced in the Articles of Association are, a line from Davenport, by way of Muscatine, to the southern or western boundary of Iowa; and northwardly, by way of Cedar Rapids, up the Cedar Valley to the north line of the State of Iowa; thus combining, in one organization, a system of railroads for central Iowa, whose eastern terminus shall be the bridge over the Mississippi River at Davenport. Those portions of these roads between Davenport and Iowa City, between Muscatine and the Junction with the M. and M. road, were completed about the first of January, and have been doing a good business.

Nothing has been done towards the Muscatine, Cedar Rapids, and Minnesota Division of the M. and M. R. R., except the pledge of stock by some of the counties along the line; but if a practicable route, and the company put their hands to the work, the road will be speedily built.

The Chief Engineer says of the country, "In November, 1854, in company with John B. Jervis, Esq., Consulting Engineer, James Archibald, Esq., a distinguished engineer, General George B. Sargeant, of Davenport, and the Hon. N. B. Judd, of Chicago, I passed over the line from Iowa City to Fort Des Moines, and thence down the 'divide' between the Des Moines and Skunk, to Oskaloosa, and from Oskaloosa, through Keokuk, Washington, and Louisa Counties, to Muscatine. The whole country on both routes is one of unsurpassed beauty and fertility. Since then, I have passed over the line from Muscatine to Cedar Rapids. No more beautiful or productive region of country can be

Mississippi Railroad Bridge, between Rock Island and Davenport.

found in the Union. There is literally no waste land to be found, and the settlements are such that a railroad would be immediately productive. The entire land on each of the routes from Davenport to Fort Des Moines, from Muscatine to Oskaloosa, and from Muscatine to Cedar Rapids, has been all purchased of the Government, and the State of Iowa is settling with a rapidity unparalleled in the history of any State."

The Mississippi Bridge, at Davenport, connects the Chicago and Rock Island, and the Mississippi and Missouri railroads; making one continuous line, without interruption or break of guage, from Chicago to the Missouri River. The people of Iowa, Western Minnesota, and those who are to cultivate the fertile soil of Nebraska, will never consent to be shut out from the Atlantic and the great Western lakes by any pretended obstruction which a bridge built on the plan proposed may offer. The bridge spans the Mississippi on the Rapids, where the current is compressed to a narrow space, so that boats, to strike the piers on either side, will first have to surmount rocks which Nature has had fixed as impediments to navigation for centuries, and of which the proposed improvement of the Rapids does not contemplate the removal. Simply a skeleton railroad bridge, the draw will always be up, save when the cars are actually crossing; which never can occur when a steamboat is passing, except by the grossest negligence. For the reasons thus concisely given, we argue that this bridge will prove no obstruction to the navigation of the river.

The estimated cost of the before-mentioned lines, for grading and bridging, track superstructure, equipments, station buildings, engineering and contingencies, are as follows:

Division.	Dist. Miles.	Cost.	Average per Mile.
Davenport to Iowa City......	54·92	$1,516,790·00	$27,618·00
Iowa City to Fort Des Moines	119·00	3,554,870·00	29,873.00
Muscatine to Oskaloosa......	95·27	2,557,500·00	26,845.00
Muscatine to Cedar Rapids..	62·64	1,493,250·00	23,839.00
Making, in the aggregate,		$9,122,410·00	

Several other railroad lines are proposed, and in part under contract, which we will mention:

The Burlington and Missouri River Railroad, being a continuation of the Chicago and Burlington Railroad, passes west, through the centres of Henry, Jefferson, Wapello, Monroe, Lucas, Clarke, Union, Adams, Montgomery, and Mills Counties, striking the Missouri opposite the mouth of the Big Platte, or Nebraska River, some twenty-five miles below Council Bluffs. This road is under contract to Wapello County, and the prospects of an early completion are good. Burlington has recently had railroad connection with Chicago, "through by daylight."

The Northern Iowa Railroad, a continuation of the Illinois Central, is projected from Dubuque west, through the Counties of Dubuque, Delaware, Buchanan, Blackhawk, Grundy, Hardin, Webster, Calhoun, Sac, Ida, and Woodbury, striking the Missouri at Sergeant's Bluffs, at the mouth of the Big Sioux River. A branch of this road is also projected to run from Delhi, in Delaware County, north, through Clayton, Fayette, and Winnesheik, to St. Paul, Minnesota. The Trunk road is called "Dubuque and Pacific."

The Des Moines Valley Railroad is to leave the Mississippi at Keokuk, passing through Lee, Van Buren, Jefferson, Wapello, Mahaska, Marion, and Jasper, to Fort Des Moines, there connecting with two east and west lines. This is considered by many as being one of the most important routes, as the Des Moines Valley, in mineral and agricultural productions, is the richest valley in the State. This road is under contract to Ottumwa.

Two lines of railroad are being built, to connect with the Galena and Chicago Union Railroad, which terminates at Fulton, Ill., on the Mississippi River. One of these, the Chicago, Iowa, and Nebraska Railroad is to run west from the new town of Clinton (2½ miles below Lyons), through Clinton, Cedar, and Linn Counties, to Cedar Rapids. This, their first Division, is to be completed and running to the west bank of the Wapsis' River, 40 miles, by the 1st of November, 1856, and to Cedar Rapids within two years. Thence this road is to continue through Benton, Tama, Grundy, Hardin, and Webster, to Fort Dodge, thence to the Missouri River. Besides this, the Iowa Central Air Line Company have their road contracted to be built from Lyons City on the Mississippi, through Maquoketa, Wyoming, Anamosa and Marion to Cedar Rapids. This is the first division of their road, and they expect to have it graded to Cedar Rapids during the present year. Thence, this road is projected to run through the middle tier of counties, to the Missouri in Monona County.

The following Table of distances exhibits the advantages possessed by these roads:

From		via		to	Miles.
From	Iowa City,	via	Junction and Davenport,	to Chicago	242
"	"	"	Clinton	"	202
"	Cedar Rapids,	"	Iowa City and Davenport,	"	267
"	"	"	Tipton, Junction, "	"	254
"	"	"	Marion, Anamosa, and Maquoketa	"	223
"	"	"	Detroit and Clinton	"	209
"	Muscatine,	"	Junction and Davenport,	"	224
"	"	"	" " Wapsipinnicon,	"	200
"	"	"	" Detroit and Clinton,	"	190

A preliminary survey has been made of a railroad from Keokuk to Davenport, *via* Montrose, West Point, Mount Pleasant, Columbus City, and Muscatine; the entire distance being 70¾ miles. The estimated cost of this road, including furniture, depôts, fencing, &c., is $1,911,934. This is one of the many roads which will seek the bridge at Davenport as the Mississippi crossing.

We doubt not that those railroad lines penetrating into the State, which are continuations of roads from the East and South, will be pushed forward to an early completion.

The construction of the several roads reaching from Chicago towards the Mississippi River demonstrates that railroads may be constructed through a country of prairie on the line of emigration, and yield a profit as soon and as far as opened. The receipts of the Chicago and Rock Island Road from the 10th of July to the 10th of January were $710,688·86. Running expenses for the same time,

$440,764·86; leaving a balance of $270,894. The whole number of passengers passing over the road for the five months ending December 1st, amounted to 168,824; total amount of freight transported during the same time, 49,734 tons.

We give the statistics of this road, because it was the first which reached the Mississippi, and reliable facts could be more easily obtained. Nor is this railroad an exception —every road to the Mississippi has paid well, as far and as fast as completed.

The Mississippi Railroad Bridge.

The great Railroad Bridge crossing the Mississippi at Davenport is steadily progressing, and will be completed and in use early this spring. Its entire length will be 5832 feet, consisting of spans of 250 feet each, exclusive of bearings. The river is divided into two channels at this point by the beautiful isle, Rock Island. The main channel is on the Iowa side, the second channel upon the Illinois side of the river. That portion of the bridge over the main channel is 1583 feet in length. The circular-shaped draw-pier, which stands near the centre of this channel, is 40 feet in height, 46 feet in diameter at the foundation, and 37 at the top.

On each side of the draw-pier is a draw of 120 feet, working on the rotary principle; making, in all, a clear space of 240 feet for the passage of river craft. These draws are open at all times, save when a train is due; and even in that case, if a boat is in sight, it will have the preference.

The average height of the bridge is 30 feet above low water.

Besides the draw-pier, there are five others. These are oblong in shape, and measure, at their base, 57 feet by 16 to 18; at their top, 24 feet by 7 to 10.

There are two abutments, one on the island and one on the Iowa shore, containing together about six thousand yards of masonry.

This bridge connects with a huge embankment, built over the lower point of the island, which lies very low, containing 125,000 cubic yards of earth, and costing forty thousand dollars. At the west end, this embankment connects with another bridge, of less dimensions, over the Illinois channel of the Mississippi. This lesser bridge has two piers, and three spans, of 150 feet each, all constructed in the same style, and upon the same principle, as those of the bridge over the main channel.

The entire length of the two bridges and the intervening embankment is 5,832 feet. The cost of the entire work will be $260,000. The bridges are being built for a single track. Their wooden work will be of pine and oak. Mr. John Warner has the contract for the masonry and grading, and Messrs. Stone and Boomer for the superstructure. The contractors are all energetic men, and are doing the work with the utmost fidelity. The bridges are built according to Howe's improved patent, and when completed will be models of strength and beauty.

This Great Bridge has naturally attracted attention from every part of the Union. The design is indeed a colossal one, and one which can only be accomplished by men of stout hearts and of iron nerve. For many long years the Mississippi has been considered an insuperable obstacle to the continuity of all great thoroughfares, from the Atlantic to the Pacific. Happily for the best interests of the West, and indeed, the whole world of commerce, a rare combination of natural facilities at this point, of the resources of modern science, of eastern capital, and of western enterprise, has made the project practicable, and insured its completion within the present year. Its opening will mark a new era in the history of Commerce, and in the annals of the Great West.

CHAPTER XIV.

RAILROAD DISTANCES ON THE VARIOUS LINES, CONNECTING CHICAGO WITH THE STATE OF IOWA.

Chicago and Rock Island Rail Road.

From Chicago to	Miles.
Junction	6
Blue Island	9
Bremen	8
Mokena	6
Joliet	11
Minooka	10
Morris	11
Seneca	10
Marseilles	5
Ottawa	8
Utica	9
La Salle	5
(Ill. Central RR. crosses).	
Peru	1
Trenton	10
Bureau Junction	4
Tiskilwa	9

Pond Creek	6
Sheffield	10
Anawan	7
Geneseo	13
Colona	10
Moline	10
Rock Island	3
Total	181

Davenport opposite side of River.

CHICAGO, BURLINGTON AND QUINCY RAIL ROAD.

From Chicago to	Miles.
Oak Ridge	8
Cottage Hill	8
Babcock's Grove	4
Danby	2
Wheaton	3
Winfield	2
Junction	3
Batavia	6
Aurora	7
Montgomery	3
Oswego	2
Bristol	3
Plano	6
Newark	5
Somonauk	3
Waverly	6
Earl	7
Mendota	11
(Crosses Illinois Central).	
Arlington	9
Dover	7
Princeton	6
Wyanet	6
French Grove	6
Nephonset	7
Kewanee	7
Galoy	8
Walnut	8
Wataga	8
Galesburg	8
Monmouth	8
Young America	8
Miss. River, opposite Burlington	18
Total	203

DISTANCES ON THE CHICAGO AND DIXON RAIL ROAD.

From Chicago to	Miles.	
Oak Ridge	8	
Cottage Hill	8	16
Babcock's Grove	4	20
Danby	2	22
Wheaton	3	25
Winfield	2	27
Junction	3	30
Geneva	5	35
Blackberry	9	44
Lodi	6	50
Courtland	5	55
De Kalb	3	58
Dement	8	66
Lane	6	72
Ogle	8	80
Franklin	7	87
Taylor	4	91
Dixon	4	96
Sterling	13	109
Union Grove	15	124
Fulton	10	134

A road is projected from Racine, Wisconsin, through Beloit, Freeport, etc., to Fulton.

As a continuation westward, two roads are being built, the "Chicago, Iowa, and Nebraska," from Clinton, and the "Iowa Central Air Line from Lyons."

DISTANCE ON THE GALENA AND CHICAGO RAIL ROAD.

From Chicago to		Miles.
Junction (See foregoing table)		30
Wayne	5	35
Clinton	4	39
Elgin	3	42
Gilbert's	8	50
Huntley's	5	55
Union	7	62
Marengo	4	66
Garden Prairie	6	72
Belvidere	6	78
Cherry Valley	6	84
Rockford	8	92
Winnebago	7	99
Pecatonica	7	106
Nevada	8	114
Freeport	7	121
Eleroy	8	129
Lena	5	134
Nora	7	141
Warren	4	145
Apple River	6	151
Scales Mound	8	159
Council Hill	5	164
Galena	7	171
Dunleith	10	181

This road is intended to connect with the Northern Iowa RR. projected from Dubuque west towards the Missouri.

DISTANCES ON THE MISSISSIPPI AND MISSOURI RAIL ROAD.

First General Division, from Davenport to Council Bluffs.

	From Davenport to	Miles.
Completed.	Wolcott	12
	Farnam	17
	Durant	20
	Junction of Muscatine and Cedar Rapids	27
	Moscow, on Cedar River	30
	West Liberty	39
	Iowa City	55
Located.	Centre of Iowa County	85
	" Poweshеik County	111
	Newton, Jasper County	141
	Fort Des Moines	174
Proposed.	Council Bluffs	310

Second General Division, from Muscatine to Mouth of Platte.

From Muscatine to		Miles.
Under Contract to Oskaloosa.	Fredonia, or Iowa River	20
	Columbus City	22
	Washington	39
	Oskaloosa	95
Surveyed.	Mouth of Platte (21 miles below Council Bluffs)	280

Third General Division, from Muscatine to Cedar Rapids.

From Muscatine to		Miles.
Graded.	Junction with 1st General Division	12
Located.	Tipton	27
	Cedar Rapids	63

DISTANCES ON THE VARIOUS STAGE ROUTES THROUGHOUT THE STATE.

DAVENPORT TO COUNCIL BLUFFS.

From Davenport to		Miles.
MUSCATINE	30	
IOWA CITY	33	63
Marengo	26	89
Sugar Grove	46	135
NEWTON	20	155
Keith's	19	174
FT. DES MOINES	14	188
Adel	24	212
Panther Creek	5	217
Bear Grove	22	239
Indian Grove	11	250
Nishnabottanny	15	265
Pleasant Spring	9	274
Indiantown	4	278
Walnut Creek	5	283
West Nishnabottany	15	298
Silver Creek	13	311
Keg Creek	6	317
COUNCIL BLUFFS	10	327

BURLINGTON TO COUNCIL BLUFFS.

From Burlington to		Miles.
London	20	
MT. PLEASANT	10	30
Rome	8	38
FAIRFIELD	15	53
Libertyville	7	60
Agency City	15	75
OTTUMWA	4	79
EDDYVILLE	15	94
OSKALOOSA	10	104
PELLA	18	122
FT. DES MOINES	46	168
See preceding table for intermediate distance.		
Council Bluffs	139	307

From Lyons and Clinton

	Miles.	
To Detroit	20	
Maquoketa	20	40
To Maquoketa direct.	35	
Wyoming	18	53
Anamosa	18	71
Marion	17	88
Cedar Rapids	6	94
To Detroit	20	
Tipton	35	55
Iowa City	25	80
To Camanche	6	
Princeton	11	17
Le Claire	6	23
Davenport	15	38
To Sabula	17	
Bellevue	20	37
Dubuque	25	62

Davenport to Dubuque.

From Davenport to	Miles.	
Dewitt	21	
Maquoketa	19	40
Andrew	8	48
La Motte	10	58
Dubuque	16	74

Dubuque to Cedar Falls.

From Dubuque to	Miles.	
Delhi	36	
Independence	36	72
Cedar Falls	25	97

9*

Dubuque to Iowa City.

From Dubuque to	Miles.	
Cascade	26	
Monticello	12	38
Anamosa	13	51
Fairview	4	55
Marion	15	70
Cedar Rapids	5	75
Iowa City	25	100

Cedar Rapids to Cedar Falls.

From Cedar Rapids to	Miles.	
Vinton	25	
Waterloo	30	65
Cedar Falls	7	72

Keokuk to Iowa City.

From Keokuk to	Miles.	
Charleston	18	
Primrose	12	30
Birmingham	24	54
Fairfield	9	63
Brighton	12	75
Washington	15	90
Iowa City	35	125

Keokuk to Keosauqua.

From Keokuk to	Miles.	
Charleston	18	
Warren	6	24
Bonaparte	12	36
Keosauqua	12	48

Bonaparte to Birmingham.

From Bonaparte to	Miles.	
Winchester	12	
Birmingham	3	15

OTTUMWA TO CHARITON.

From Ottumwa to		Miles.
Albin	25	
Chariton	25	50

OSKALOOSA TO COUNCIL BLUFFS.

From Oskaloosa to		Miles.
Knoxville	25	
Indianola	25	50
Wintersett	25	75
Lewis	70	145
Council Bluffs	60	205

FAIRFIELD TO KEOSAQUA, 20

MUSCATINE TO BURLINGTON.

From Muscatine to		Miles.
Grandview	14	
Wapello	10	24
Linton	9	33
Burlington	19	52

RIVER DISTANCES.

MISSISSIPPI RIVER.

From St. Louis to	Miles.
Alton	22
Grafton	18
Milan	24
Wiota	42
Worthington	52
Westport	57
Hamburg	62
Clarksville	80
Louisiana	82
Scott's Landing	97
Cincinnati	105
Saverton	115
Hannibal	123
Marion City	133
Quincy	143
La Grange	155
Smoot's Landing	159
Canton	161
Tully	163
Gregory's Landing	175
Alexandria	185
Keokuk	190
Nashville	198
Montrose	202
Nauvoo	204
Fort Madison	214
Pontoosuc	220
Burlington	235
Oquawka	250
Keithsburg	262
New Boston	269
Muscatine 299 Drury	304
Salem	309
Buffalo and Andalusia	321
Rockingham	329
R. Island and Davenport	334
Hampton	346
Port Byron 353 Cordova	358
Camanche 364 N. Albany	367
Clinton, Terminus C. I. & N. R. R.	375
Fulton, Terminus G. & C. U. R. R.	376
Lyons, Terminus I. C. A. R. R.	377
Sabula 395 Savannah	397
Bellevue 412 Galena	428
Dubuque and Dunleith	453

Peru (Iowa)	461
Cassville	484
Guttenburg	498
Clayton City	508
Wyoming	513
Wisconsin river	517
McGregor's Landing	521
Fort Crawford	523
Prairie du Chien	524
Lansing	559
Winnesheik	579
Warner's Landing	589
Prairie La Cross	617
Mouth of Black river	629
Reed's Landing	637
Wabashaw	705
Lake Pepin	708
Red Wing	736
Mouth of Lake St. Croix	786
Red Rock	803
Little Crow Village	805
St. Paul	809
Mendotah	819
St. Peter	823

MISSOURI RIVER.

From Alton to	Miles.
Mouth of Missouri	7
St. Charles	34
Mt. Auburn	64
Augusta	69
South Point	76
Washington	85
Pinckney	94
Hermann	109
Portland	119
St. Aubert	139
Bennett's Landing	149
Mouth of Osage	152
Jefferson City	162
Claysville	169
Marion	174
Nashville	187
Providence	189
Rocheport	201
Boonville	211
Arrow Rock	226
Glasgow	241
Cambridge	249
Keytesville Landing	256
Brunswick	275
Dewitt	287
Miami	293
Hill's Landing	313
Waverly	319
Dover Landing	331
Lexington	343
Wellington	354
Camden	364
Napoleon	372
Sibley	379
Richfield	394
Blue Mills Landing	404
Liberty	414
Wayne City	420
Randolph	428
Kansas	433
Parkville	448
Narrows Landing	459
Fort Leavenworth	468
Weston	475
Columbus Landing	504
St. Joseph	537
Savannah	559
Iowa Point	585
Council Bluffs	789

CHAPTER XV.

STATISTICS.

A Table showing the number of Polls, Acres of Land, and its Value, Value of Town Lots, Value of Capital employed in Merchandising, also in Manufacturing. Number and Value of Horses, Cattle, and of all other property (except Mules, Sheep, and Hogs, assessed in the Counties in the year 1854.

Counties.	No. of polls.	Acres of land.	Val. of Land with improvement.	Value of town lots.	Val. of capital employed in merchandise.	Val. of capital employed in manufacturing.	Horses.		No. of cattle.	Value of cattle.	Value of all other property.	Total value.	Total value in 1853.
							No.	Value.					
Adair,													
Adams,		6,659	$15.006	$2,517			67	$3,390	356	$7.089	$6.973	$35,454	
Appanoose,	844	191,634	628,308	28,922	$21,501	$4,525	1,396	74,055	5,016	77,145	41,189	891,325	$584,915
Alamakee,	784	198,651	473,106	49 344	22,100	1,500	552	36,795	3,795	70,036	36,146	700,794	429 371
Benton,	400	113,076	472,685	19,404			764	47,271	2,093	26,535	51.620	637 809	265,574
Blackhawk,	500	88,903	379,724	48,678			361	18.503	1,189	22,211	43,753	515,802	97,478
Boone,	330	63,419	225,180	6,915	8,303	2,600	468	23.535	1,305	22,345	26,485	322,663	147,931
Bremer,	234	81,406	208,751	8,625	5,140	7,450	362	13,184	1,025	16,537	20,219	285.056	43,437
Buchanan,	500	107,750	358,003	59,115	16,701	9,161	686	43,151	2,383	40,703	63,675	598.495	264,885
Butler,		9,029	33,381	500			111	5,645	489	9,141	6,591	56,411	
Cass,											Estimated,	80 000	57.968
Clarke,	272	81,600	263.571	8,185	3.918		381	20,335	1,315	25,232	28,530	354,744	117,616
Cedar,	1,263	335,237	1,646.563	79,162	26.999	7,241	2,870	164,203	7,679	116,427	170.264	2,246,516	1,244,040
Chickasaw,	97	78.727	191,448	2.754	4,067		81	3,681	472	6,625	6,450	216,154	
Clayton,	1,492	316,712	1,149,478	267.879	62,965	27,261	1,820	115,889	7,431	157,084	107,475	1,916,334	1,350.066
Clinton,	1,076	356,063	1,450 678	214,725	37,373	8,700	1,937	119.063	7,627	125,554	75,113	2,051,712	1,033.076
Dallas,	304	100.107	319,555	6,112	2,575	4,700	745	35,150	2,136	32,078	45 083	457.634	228.114
Davis,	1,742	251,383	771,608	70,229			2,939	125,092	9,471	119,776	191,092	1,306,700	1,162,133
Decatur,	426	91,769	244,498	5,242			758	36.503	3,128	44.781	61,128	403.866	149,801
Delaware,	818	237,100	572,614	27,710	15,250		1,175	55 248	4,316	60,863	64,239	803,738	544,222
Des Moines,	2,644	238,431	2,069,382	1,244,634	274,897	38,330	4,338	210,986	14,841	174,464	380,172	4,470.333	4,214,245
Dubuque,											Estimated,	5,000,000	4,148,387
Fayette,	696	180,000	450,000	50,000	66,848	14,850	457	28,873	3,228	52,068	12,200	683,124	342,178
Fremont,	412	47,153	219,664	13,924	18,917	1,400	878	44,102	4,190	55,713	33.497	397,046	101,576
Guthrie,	159	33,670	120,425	4,613	2,815	1,780	248	13,222	857	13,603	16,521	176,117	57,421

Greene,		7,700	16,546				68	3,235	198	5,541	12,651	39,074	
Hardin,	169	19,844	34,403	1,375	1,810		186	8,080	199	10,907	16,641	75,592	
Harrison,											Estimated,	50,000	
Henry,	1,850	259,963	1,436,607	243,574	71,937	19,218	3,320	161,193	10,310	125,429	219,800	2,328,010	1,936,806
Iowa,	346	133,453	519,111	6,474	7,200	1,150	638	35,824	2,000	33,063	42,291	657,022	337,175
Jackson,	2,162	368,802	1,535,841	196,702	57,520	6,968	3,189	184 902	11,273	185,620	138,166	2,350,441	2,023,627
Johnson,	1,448	347,952	1,606,626	478,910	67,442	10 988	2,474	139,566	7,592	121,066	185,195	2,645,148	1,684,430
Jones,	968	237,699	757,225	31,615	15,651	1,747	1,808	99,071	6,061	89,767	56,731	1,076,848	863,879
Jasper,	563	192,510	661,969	46,305	12,250	9,200	1,202	64,055	3,158	52,805	104,222	966,620	447,651
Jefferson,	1,778	266,606	954,537	135,859	44,375	6.567	3,655	136,749	12,035	120.974	164,469	1,609,892	1,372.917
Keokuk,	1,235	304,696	1,179,557	35,794	41,045	10,408	2,186	109,974	7,202	108,770	136,838	1,659,154	918,607
Lee,	3,753	318,500	2,191,721	1,487 345	374,326	34,891	5,372	281,889	17,839	224,579	545,385	5,306,732	4,195,365
Linn,	1,628	332,726	1,720,529	335,038	63,225	19,800	3,414	206,882	8,856	137,199	185.458	2,753,459	1,766,899
Lucas,											Estimated,	300,000	211.887
Louisa,	1,007	219,156	1,267,068	95 070	47,583	12,775	2,439	132,194	8,998	114,186	164,686	1,883 619	1,361,674
Madison,	487	163,115	553,384	34,300	13,850		878	45.151	2,856	41,942	49,640	750,586	320 906
Mahaska,	1,691	237,089	1,137,011	185,312	59,643	21,094	3,177	159,998	10,834	124,138	195 399	2,034,983	1,620.064
Marion,	1,687	229,391	1,029,816	110,741	62,506	16,105	2,650	136,463	8,674	129,194	128,816	1,650,578	1,060,496
Mills,	366	55,575	169,310	14,279	32,885	2,430	697	35.039	2,746	39,686	29,661	332,454	104,355
Monroe,	728	130,342	469,450	25,633	16,918	1,735	1,282	64,298	4,217	63.951	67,170	732,116	519,666
Montgomery,	26	3,127	5,363		90		45	2,720	201	4,561	2,405	16,539	
Monona,	24						25	1,400	489	8,593	2.576	12,810	
Marshall,	272	64,172	268,841	11,008	5,555	1,270	471	25,517	1,342	21,593	21,953	360,849	124,296
Muscatine,	1,384	247,190	1,768,060	877,530	154,560	23,007	2,611	144,961	7,757	109 112	184,149	3,286,534	2,114,932
Page,	171	15,855	39,363	565	4.952	1,500	412	17,905	1,110	20,893	18,121	109.518	47,458
Polk,	916	198,092	934,913	129.180	43,845	15,150	1,595	64.189	4,461	62,314	113,344	1,386,309	1,017,382
Pottawatamie,	507	48,565	131,396	121,413	233.626		620	37,595	3,4 3	52,999	52,643	637,820	150,728
Powashiek,	350	147,278	614,132	8,718	2,600		588	20,574	1,983	25,595	36,749	716,621	189,875
Scott,	1,616	307,200	2,533,853		129,573	22,619	2,841	151 525	11,137	128,745	839,746	3,841,116	2,840,914
Story,	146	38,236	96.876	727	600		196	9,539	686	11,270	11,138	132,557	46,651
Shelby,	59	720	1,390				69	4,600	446	7,887	1,937	22,643	
Tama,	174	73,993	218,883	1,018	682		266	12,807	1,044	17,701	21,663	276,605	81,403
Taylor,											Estimated,	40,000	22,582
Van Buren,	2,471	310,645	1,606,520		67,468	36,669	4,207	184.637	12,534	138,792	212,127	2,302,675	2,101,426
Union,		3,012	7,233				11	695	82	1,696	541	10,496	
Washington,	1,498	274,134	1,262,143	95,482	45,605	18,439	2.709	50,729	8,509	131,501	200,687	1,851,639	1,180,190
Wayne,		41,990	89,081	3,259			374	19,572	1,378	21,628	25,720	166,731	117,580
Wapello,	1,502	216,584	864,124	149,692	52,504	8,673	3,054	132,969	9,003	115,249	167,816	1,538,308	1,313,801
Warren,											Estimated,	800,000	619,180
Webster,		18 567	58,748	720			143	7,035	632	9.223	10,680	89,164	20,658
Winneshiek,	663	152,099	670,277	20,631	17,200	3,630	500	32,665	3,441	72,118	48,754	875,066	210,610
Woodbury,											Estimated,	40,000	
	48,675	9,175,097	$40,772,532	$6,564,458	$2,359,504	$1,639,411	82 586	$4,164,762	279.977	$3,966,277	$5,904.278	$72,327,204	$49,540,304
In 1853,	27,620	6,977,192	27,527,106	3,108,002	1,231,704	253,464	73,558	3,218,759	243,730	2,856,538	4,217,482	49,549,304	
Increase in 1 yr.	21,055	2,197,905	$13,245,426	$3 456,456	$1,127,800	$385,947	9.028	$946.003	36.247	$1,109,639	$1,686,796	$22,786,900	

The following items are omitted in the preceding Table, but included in the "Total Value" column:—

No. of Mules in the State	2,232
Value " " "	116,955
No. of Sheep " "	169,542
Value " " "	204,061
No. of Hogs " "	611,923
Value " " "	873,103

The increase in value of property in any county for the past year, can be ascertained by comparing the items of the counties, in the two total columns, for 1853 and 1854.

Financial.

State Revenue on hand, Nov. 1, 1852	$8,602 88
Receipts from above date up to Oct. 31, 1854	114,946 87
Proceeds from Sale of Saline Lands up to Oct. 31, 1854	10,515 70
Total amount of Receipts	$134,065 45
During the same period there has been paid out on Auditor's Warrants	118,542 90
Leaving a balance in Treasury of	$15,522 55

An estimate of the necessary expenditures for the two years, commencing Nov. 1st, 1854, and ending October 31, 1856:—

Agricultural Societies	$5,000,00
Governor, Superintendent, Secretary, Auditor, Attorney-General, Treasurer, and Librarian's salaries	9,300 00
Blind Asylum	6,000 00
Deaf and Dumb	4,000 00
Carried over	$24,300 00

Brought over	$24,300 00
Funded debt—bonds now due	16,442 00
General contingent fund	2,000 00
Interest account	13,000 00
Judges' salary	24,000 00
Miscellaneous disbursements	6,000 00
Penitentiary	6,000 00
Supreme Court expenses	2,[illegible]0 00
State printing	7,[illegible]00 00
State officers' contingent fund	3,000 00
State House	6,000 00
Stationery	5,000 00
Legislative expenses and other special appropriations	25,000 00
	$139,742 00

CHAPTER XVI.

DESCRIPTION OF COUNTIES.

To describe minutely and separately counties that possess so nearly the same qualities as do those situated adjacent to each other, in any portion of this State, would be a useless task; hence, where a full description is given of the soil, productions, climate, &c., of one county, and those adjoining are very similar, the description is not repeated. For instance, the general description of Winneshiek County, answers for every adjoining county in the north-east, Henry or Jefferson for the south-east, Pottawattamie for the west, Scott and Jackson for the east, and so on.

ADAMS COUNTY

At the present time has a population of 1100. Last census, 342. Quincy, the county-seat, contains 150 inhabitants, and one district school under common school law. An Academy, or College, under the patronage of the Methodist Episcopal Church, is in progress of construction: they have as yet but one teacher in the primary department. There are no manufactories in operation. A steam saw and grist-mill, and carding and fulling-mills are very much needed. Tailors, blacksmiths, saddlers, coopers, wagon makers, etc., are much wanted.

The price of land adjoining the town is from $8 to $20 per acre. There is no other town in the county.

The Icarian Society (a branch of the Nauvoo Society, Illinois,) is located 6 miles south-east of Quincy; they number some 60 inhabitants, live on the community plan —all eating at one table—the different families having separate houses to live in. Their village is situated on the east side of the East Nodaway, occupying a beautiful timbered knoll, as the State road from Chariton to Glenwood leaves the bottom for the high prairie. Their houses are built very compact, on two principal streets.

Nineteen hundred acres of heavily-timbered school land, in the northern part of the county, will be in market during 1856. Good prairie land can be had in this county, at $1.25 per acre, and timber land can be bought at from $5 to $15 per acre, as to quality and location. This county is out of debt, and it has a neat new court-house. Total levy of taxes for 1855, including State, County, School, Road, and a special Bridge Tax, amounted to only 8½ mills on the dollar. This year they will be much less. Veins of stone coal, 2½ to 3½ feet thick, have been found along the Middle Nodaway.

No soil in the world will stand as much dry weather as this, and there is none that is less injured by continued wet weather. Owing to these peculiarities of the climate, no section of country can compare with this for stock raising. On the north is

ADAIR COUNTY,

Of which Somerset is the county-seat, and Adair, Alcora's, Holaday's, Marvin's, and Wahtahwah post-offices. Directly northwest lies

AUDUBON COUNTY,

Organized in April, 1855, Dayton being located as the seat of justice. There are post-offices and settlements known as Ballard's, Bear Grove, Hamlin Grove, and Big Grove.

These counties are well watered and have a good proportion of prairie and timber. Audubon, though comprising only 12 townships, has upwards of 7000 acres of timber land.

APPANOOSE COUNTY

Is well watered by the Chariton and its tributaries, furnishing power for numerous mill sites. Timber, about an average; soil, excellent; climate, mild and pleasant. Centreville is the county-seat.

ALAMAKEE COUNTY

Is bounded on the east by the Mississippi River. It is the extreme N. E. county of the State. The first settlements made by whites were in 1850. The present population of the county numbers some 8000.

The principal towns are Lansing, 1000; Wawkon, 350; and Paint Rock, 100 inhabitants. Church edifices and school-houses are being erected throughout the county with great liberality.

Alamakee may well pride herself on the increase in population and importance she made last year.

In March, 1855, there were but six saw-mills and two grist-mills in the county. Now (Jan., 1856), there are 15 water, and 3 steam saw-mills, and 11 grist-mills, all successfully and profitably operating. Manufactories of farming utensils, cooperage, &c., are much needed. The facilities for getting pine lumber are good, and oak, lynn, and black walnut are plenty.

BENTON COUNTY

Was first settled by S. M. Lockhart, in the spring of 1841; soon after, other families followed. In August, 1851, C. C. Charles's was the only family that resided in what is now Vinton. The reports of the assessors in regard to this, as well as many other sections, are very incorrect. In 1855 they gave Vinton 307—now there are 600. The county was censused at 2623, but at that time there were at least 3000, and the population of Benton is now fully 4000.

The O. S. and N. S. Presbyterians have established societies, and are preparing to erect churches.

One school, well conducted, with 90 scholars.

One steam saw-mill, cutting 4000 feet of lumber every 24 hours. A flouring-mill is very much needed.

This county is well watered, with a due proportion of prairie and timber.

The settlements of the county are at Burk's P. O., Marysville, Beulah P. O., Taylor's Creek P. O., and Prairie Creek P. O. Benton City, 300 inhabitants.

BLACK HAWK COUNTY.

This county, bearing the name of the illustrious chief, possesses some of the finest soil and timber land in Northern Iowa. It is in the same range with, and the third county from, Dubuque. The Cedar fork of the Iowa river passes diagonally in a south-easterly direction across the county. Cedar Falls is a town of considerable importance, and will become a large manufacturing place. At this, as well as several other points in the county, the best of water-power and eligible sites for mills and manufacturing establishments hold out inducements to capitalists. In August, 1855, the county-seat was removed to Waterloo, which is improving rapidly, and is permanently and advantageously located.

BOONE COUNTY

Was first settled at Pea's Point, (now called Flat-rock,) in May, 1846, by John Pea, a pioneer of the old stock, a Pennsylvanian by birth, who has lived in every State that intervenes between his native State and Iowa, when they were wild and primitive forests. He was also an early settler in Missouri. This old man still resides in Boone County, and with the gray hairs of some seventy years upon his head, such are his erect form and comparatively robust constitution, that Time seems to have broken its billows over his manly form, only as the ocean reads its fury over the immovable rock of its shores. The old gentleman is still full of adventure and enterprise, and may ere long be one of the freemen of Nebraska.

Montgomery McCall settled near where Boonsboro now stands, in the month of February, 1847, and for about a year his family lived nearer the source of the Des Moines river than any other white family. During the winter of 1846 and 1847, seven hundred Pottawattamie Indians were encamped in the vicinity of these families.

The town of Boonsboro was located on the 7th day of July, 1851, as the county-seat, by commissioners appointed for that purpose by the State Legislature, and is likely ever to remain the seat of justice for the county.

The present population of Boonsboro is about 450. The population of the county over 2000. Immigration is rapidly pouring in.

The following named towns, recently laid out, have the

population annexed. Sweet Point, 250; Rapids, 100; Ridgeport, 75; Milford, 75; Carsonsport, 50; Quincy, 25.

Since July, 1855, steam saw-mills have been erected at Boonsboro, Milford, and Sweet Point—all doing well, and still there is room.

In Boone, as in every other county in the State, mechanics of every kind are in demand, wages high and employment constant.

BREMER COUNTY

Was settled first in 1848–9. In the spring of 1853, the town of Janesville, six miles below Waverly, was laid out by John T. Barrie. This town is situated on the east bank of the Cedar River, some three miles above the junction of the Cedar and the Shellrock. The place contains some 150 inhabitants, with two stores, saw-mill, &c. A flouring-mill is much needed, and the water-power along these streams is sufficient to furnish sites for all the machinery needed. A great abundance of building-stone and the best of timber admirably fit this for a manufacturing place.

But one school in Janesville — a fine stone school-house is now being erected, 24 by 36 feet.

The M. E. Church are making arrangements to build a house of worship this season. There are one stationary and two local itinerant ministers; the churches are well attended and prosperous.

In June, 1853, the county-seat was located six miles above Janesville, on the east bank of the Cedar River, and the town of Waverly established, which has now a population of some 450. Population increased 350 in eighteen months. The population of Bremer County is about 3000. Public schools in every settlement through the county. A body of timber, known as "the lower big woods," embracing some 40 sections, lies in the vicinity of these towns, which, in a prairie country, is a consideration of no minor importance. This is a healthy and productive region of country, possessing beautifnl scenery, and excellent agricultural and manufacturing advantages.

BUCHANAN COUNTY

Was first settled by Ezra G. Allen and Wm. Bennett, in 1842.

Independence, the county-seat, was located and settled in the winter of 1846, by Rufus Blelark.

Present population of the town, 700—of the county, 3500.

No church buildings erected. One is being erected at Independence, and one at Quasqueton.

No newspaper in the county. Two flouring-mills (two burrs each), and two saw-mills, are in operation in the county.

Woollen manufactories most needed, there being none within 40 miles.

Oak timber plenty along the streams, and deep-soiled rolling prairies between the water-courses. The streams are rather rapid, with gravelly or rocky beds. Limestone abundant. Soil generally rich sandy loam.

CARROLL COUNTY

Was to have been organized in March of the present year. The present population of the county is but about 250. Water-power, timber lands, and the best of prairie soil, with inexhaustible beds of building-stone, coal, and iron, are some of the inducements Carroll County holds out to new-comers. As yet no towns are laid out, not even the county-seat, and the active, intelligent, and ambitious immigrant will find inducements for settling in recently-organized counties which do not exist in older ones. Though water-power is afforded by several streams in various parts of the county, there is not a mill or manufactory yet erected, and the nearest mill is at Panora, Guthrie County, 27 miles distant. What an opening for a saw and grist-mill! Wheat, corn, and rye in abundance. Of churches and schools in Carroll we could obtain no information, and presume that they, like the county, are unorganized.

CASS COUNTY

Joins Pottawattamie on the east, and, like those adjoining on the west and south, was settled by Mormons in 1846–7, who, however, left in the spring of 1852, when W. L. Townsend, P. Hedges, J. Bradshaw, C. E. Woodward, George Reeves, and J. W. Benedict took their places, and became permanent settlers.

Lewis, the county-seat, was first settled by R. C. Lambert. The population of the county is now a little rising of 700. A fine court-house is to be built in Lewis this season.

There is but one church in Lewis — occupied by the Congregationalists and Methodists.

No newspaper, but one needed.

Two good common schools in Lewis, in very good condition.

Two saw-mills and one grist-mill. A woollen factory would do well, also mechanics of every kind — blacksmiths, plough and wagon makers, cabinet-makers, and day laborers.

Cass County is unsurpassed, in point of fertility and water, in the State,— is well supplied with timber and stone. The soil gently undulating and dry. There is now but little unentered land in this county.

CEDAR COUNTY

Was organized and settled in 1836. The county-seat, Tipton, was laid out in 1839. Present population of the town 800, and of the county about 8700.

The towns and settlements in the county are Tipton, Woodridge, Cedar Bluffs, Pioneer P. O., Cedar P. O., Massillon P. O., Yankee Grove P. O., Red Oak P. O., Gower's P. O., Inland P. O., Springdale P. O., Padee P. O., Lacton P. O., and Rochester.

Three churches in Tipton—Presbyterian, Congregational, and Methodist,—society very good. Churches of different denominations throughout the county, but the precise number of church edifices or members not ascertained.

A railroad line from the Muscatine junction of the Mississippi and Missouri Railroad to Tipton, is projected; and it is probable that the Chicago, Iowa and Nebraska Railroad, (passing west from Clinton on the Mississippi,) will be completed as far as Tipton, during the present year. One of these roads will be built, and probably both, which will give Tipton an impetus in importance and wealth, known only to similarly favoured cities in the West.

The county is made up of very excellent soil, adapted to all kinds of farming purposes, and well watered generally. Timber is less abundant in Cedar than in many other counties. Yet taken as a whole, Cedar holds out strong inducements to the farmer and mechanic, to locate within her borders.

CHICKASAW COUNTY.

Four years ago Chickasaw County had not a single white resident—now the population of the county exceeds 1500. In 1853, Rufus Clark, a famous trapper and hunter, a native of Ohio, settled in the vicinity of the present Bradford P. O., which is in the neighbourhood of the junction of the Little and the Big Cedar Rivers. The population of Bradford now is 300. One district school with an average attendance of 70 scholars. Preaching every Sabbath—principally Methodist. No churches organized yet.

Two saw-mills in full operation, and a steam saw-mill being erected.

Capitalists and traders would find this a wide and inviting field for their operations.

Flouring-mill much needed. Flour is now brought 45 miles, and grain taken the same distance to mill. With any amount of water-power all over the county, and the best of grain soil, we hope some capitalist will consult his interest by contributing to the wants of the people of Chickasaw.

CLARKE COUNTY

Was first settled in 1849. In 1850, according to the census, it contained 79 inhabitants. The population of the county now, (February, 1856), numbers upwards of 3000. The county-seat, Osceola, was settled in 1852—present population, 200.

There are no church buildings erected in the county as yet; but the Methodists, Campbellites, and United Brethren have each an organization.

CLAYTON COUNTY

Is the most northern river county in the State, except Alamakee. It is bounded on the east by the Mississippi, on the west by Fayette, on the south by Delaware and Dubuque. The principal water-courses in the county are Yellow and Turkey Rivers, Volga and Buck Creeks, and Bloody Run. Turkey River is among the most beautiful and placid streams in the State, and is celebrated for its numerous geological specimens, and the picturesque scenery of its banks and dells. Turkey River affords most excellent water-power for mills and machinery, and is navigable the greater part of the year, as far up as the forks. The soil is about the same as in those counties adjoining, already described.

CLINTON COUNTY.

WAS first settled in 1836, by Mr. Bourne, who located upon Sec. 1, T. 80, R. 4, East. The county was surveyed in 1837, by the Messrs. Burtz. The Surveyor General's office was then at Cincinnati, Ohio. In 1840, the county was organized by Sheriff Bourne. In 1841, R. R. Bedford and others formed a little settlement at De Witt, and during the same year Messrs. Wheeler and Evans erected a log court-house. In stepping from the past to the present, we quote the language of one of the "oldest inhabitants." He says: "Clinton County was originally settled by the poorest class of people on God's earth; and it is with great pleasure that I have witnessed their progress, slow but sure, and now find the most of them very comfortably situated."

Although this county is, in many respects, more favourably situated than any other in the State, but little has been known of it at home or abroad, until quite recently, owing to the fact that, the great tide of travel passed over the railroads to the Mississippi, entering the State at Dubuque, Davenport, or Burlington, and striking thence directly to Iowa City, or Ft. Des Moines, virtually running around Clinton and Jackson counties. Since the completion of the railroad to Fulton, a good proportion of the eastern travel has passed over this road, entering the State at Clinton or Lyons—thus reaching the Mississippi with fifty miles less travel than by any other railroad route. Convinced of the rapid advance and increase in population and property that awaits this point, capitalists, mechanics, and business men, are daily investing in lands and town lots, and entering into business, which will largely contribute to the credit of the County and the State. As will be seen by reference to the map, or to the list of post-offices, there are comparatively few towns in Clinton County, and although rapidly advancing, property of all kinds is much cheaper than at any other railroad terminus on the River.

The "Lyons Iowa Central Railroad Company," which some years since projected a road west from Lyons, through Tipton and Iowa City, after making a fair beginning upon the work, in consequence of the financial crisis, failed. Their stock, bonds, &c., were purchased at sheriff's sale, by a number of gentlemen of reliability and reputation, who have organized a new company under the name of the "Chicago, Iowa and Nebraska Railroad Company." For numerous and satisfactory reasons, they fixed upon a point two miles below Lyons, as the eastern terminus of their road. The "Iowa Land Company," owning the lands there, and being also interested in the new organization, laid out a town, calling it CLINTON. Their town plot, embracing 1000 lots, is laid out upon the most liberal scale. Whole blocks have been left for parks; four lots given to each of the several churches; also liberal provision for seminaries, libraries, and public schools. The original proprietors of the town grade the streets, and plant shade trees along the side-walks, at their own expense. The wide streets and avenues, the liberal policy of the proprietors, the prospect of the railroad, must, together with the unsurpassed beauty and admirable adaptation of the location for a large town, gave it a popularity which few towns of its age enjoy. In seven months from the first sale, nearly all the lots in the plot were sold to individuals who must improve them; such being the conditions of sale.

To the stranger abroad, the proximity of two growing towns, situated as Lyons and Clinton, within two miles of each other, on the banks of the Mississippi—the one opposite, the other nearly opposite to the terminus of a railroad running out of Chicago, the question would arise "which will be *the* city?" In the present embryotic state of the two places, it is natural that much petty jealousy and some rivalry must exist between the inhabitants and those particularly interested in the places; but we believe that the sentiment contained in the following toast, read at the celebration of the founding of the town of Clinton, (Aug. 1, 1855), and the commencement of the new railroad, exists among the earnest workers for the prosperity of this important point, on the Upper Mississippi:

"*Our sister city, Lyons.*—Her interests and ours are the same. In building up the waste places between us, we propose to meet her half way."

The population of this County in 1840, was 821; in 1850, 2822; in 1854, 7000; and in 1856, 11,000. The population of Lyons in 1850, was 453. Now, the population of this point, (Lyons and Clinton), is 2700!

Since the completion of the Railroad from Chicago, the produce from a large section of country finds here a ready market, which adds much to the business of the city. Several heavy produce houses will be opened in each of these

11

places, and mills are being erected in each. In Lyons, there are already in operation, 3 steam mills, and 1 foundery, and another nearly completed. A new hotel is to be built at Lyons, this season, and another at Clinton, in addition to the one just completed. This house is three stories high, large and commodious, capable of accommodating 500 persons. Several three, four, and five story brick and stone blocks are under contract in Clinton, and as many more projected in Lyons. It is thought the increase in buildings and inhabitants, at this point, in 1856, will exceed that of any other in the State.

At both Lyons and Clinton, recently, the Episcopalian and Presbyterian denominations have each organized a church, and in Lyons settled pastors. The Congregational and Methodist organizations at the former place, have been some years in existence. A fine edifice is being erected by the Episcopalian Society, at Clinton, and another for a Free Church and school building. Ex-Governor Baker, of New Hampshire, has identified himself with the place, and, with others, is making arrangements for founding (and building) a university, public library, &c. The Congregational Church, at Lyons, is just being completed, and occupies one of the most commanding and beautiful sites in this section. Other church buildings are needed, and will probably be erected this year.

This point, which has so recently been brought into notice by the completion of the Chicago and Fulton Railroad, has been richly endowed by nature with some of the most commanding views found on the Upper Mississippi. With the splendid bluff scenery, and gently sloping plains that descend to the river's brink, thickly wooded with a fine growth of scrub oak, affording beautiful and refreshing shade, may be found one of the finest locations in the world for a large city; and we predict that 1860 will find a rapidly growing city of 20,000 inhabitants—a city stretching along the Father of Waters for three miles, whose massive warehouses gather the wealth of a rich inland tract, while her magnificent bluffs are crowned by the tasteful cottage and the splendid mansion.

Camanche, eight miles below Lyons, is improving rapidly, also, and bids fair to become a town of importance. During the past year, several new and substantial brick buildings have been erected, and extensive preparations are making for building this season. Population of Camanche, 1000.

De Witt is the county-seat, and the largest interior town in the County. Being near the centre of a rapidly improving, a fast populating, a most fertile and prosperous country, De Witt holds out great inducements to those who want town property, or farms, near the first depôt west of the Mississippi, on the Iowa City Railroad.

Of newspapers, there are a Democratic and an Independent paper at Lyons, an Independent one at De Witt, and one about being established at Clinton—making 4 in the county.

Clinton consists of beautiful, rich, rolling prairie, interspersed with groves of timber. "Second-hand lands can be bought on better terms in Clinton than any county in the State, according to their true value."

Clinton contains five churches — Episcopal, Methodist, Congregational, Roman Catholic, and one union of the Baptists and Disciples.

Good public and select schools in every town of the county, and in good condition.

[NOTE.—In preparing our edition for 1855, sickness prevented us visiting, and correctly representing this county—hence we devote to it more space than we should have done, but not more than it deserves. Those wanting information not contained in this volume, either of this or any other portion of the State, will apply in person, or by letter addressed to the author, care of Parker, Dole & Co., Bankers and Land Agents, Clinton, Iowa. See card at the close of this volume.]

CALHOUN COUNTY.

This County has about six excellent townships of land, most of it in the south-west corner; about eight middling, and the balance quite swampy, particularly around the Twin Lakes. The Coon River passes through the south-west corner. Some fine groves of timber on its borders, one grove of about sixty acres near Twin Lakes, contains all the timber in the county. The county was organized at the August election. The county-seat, just located, is called Brooklin.

DALLAS COUNTY

Was first settled by Samuel Miller and family, in 1846. The population of the county, according to the last census, was 2565; its present population is 3100. Adel, the county-seat, is beautifully located on the west side of North Raccoon River.

Wiscotta is beautifully situated at the junction of South and Middle Coon Rivers, 35 miles due west from Fort Des Moines.

Five public schools in the county, all in a prosperous condition. No private schools.

Dallas has five water, and one steam, saw-mills. Grist-mills and manufactories greatly needed. The many fine streams that afford water-power in this county, and the fertile soil, producing abundant crops, call loudly to the capitalists and farmers, mechanics, and business men of every class, to examine her claims and advantages. The Railroad west from Fort Des Moines is projected to run through this county.

The country lies high, rolling, and healthy, but is comparatively sparsely settled, as the number of inhabitants indicates.

DAVIS COUNTY

Is the second county from the Mississippi, on the Missouri State line, and is settled to a great extent by immigrants from Missouri and Illinois. The principal streams watering the county are the north and south branches of the Waukindau, and the Fox River, which, with several smaller streams, have their rise in the county, passing through Missouri to the Mississippi. The Des Moines River runs diagonally across the north-east corner of the county, several of whose tributaries traverse the county. The principal towns in Davis County are Bloomfield,(the county-seat,) Troy, Drakesville, Nottingham, and Mount Calvary, and small settlements, the post-offices of which are named Oak Spring, Soap Creek, Salt Creek, Pleasant View, Taylor, Troy, Dover, Pulaski, Stringtown, Monterey, Savannah, Roscoe, and Del Norte.

For a full description of the soil see Monroe—the soil in the two counties being similar.

DES MOINES COUNTY

Was first settled in 1832, by David Tothers, who settled three miles south-west of what is now Burlington. The next settlement was made by S. S. White and Amzi Doolittle, who were the proprietors of the original town. Additions were laid out in the order in which they are named: in 1836, by David Rorer, Amos Ladd, Enoch Wade, Isaac Leffler, G. W. Kelley, and others since. Population 10,500.

There are eleven houses of worship, viz.: two Roman Catholic, one Episcopal, two Methodist Episcopal, one German Methodist, one German Lutheran, one Congregational, one Baptist, and one Presbyterian. There are also three congregations who intend erecting houses of worship soon, viz.: Second Presbyterian, Cumberland Presbyterian, and Christian.

"Iowa State Gazette," weekly and tri-weekly; "Hawkeye," same; and the "Telegraph," daily and weekly, are published in this county.

Two large public school-houses, costing over $4000 each, in which eight schools are taught. There are also quite a number of private schools, all in a flourishing condition; and the Baptist University, of which an account is published on another page. (See Chapter on *Education.*)

They have two machine and engine manufactories, two foundries, one planing mill, two steam flouring-mills, four sash, door and blind factories, three steam saw-mills, one shingle factory, one steam match factory, two furniture manufactories; two coach, five wagon, two plough, one brush, one candle, and one starch factory; two large pork packing establishments, three banking houses, six hotels, three plank roads. Railroad connection with Chicago. Burlington and Missouri River railroad will be finished to Mt. Pleasant this summer—almost entirely graded to Ottumwa now. They have several large bakeries. An oil and paper mill no doubt would do well there.

The opening of the railroad between Chicago and Burlington has given a new impetus to the latter city, and the population and business of the place increased more during the past year than it has in any three years previous.

The people of Burlington are industrious and energetic, and their intelligence and literary taste may be judged of from the fact that the most extensive, if not the only Historical and Geological Society of the State, is located at this place. We are indebted to one of its gentlemanly members for a brief history of this institution, which follows:—

"The *Iowa Historical and Geological Institute* was organized December 18th, 1843, and incorporated December 31st, 1850. Its effects were destroyed by fire, January 16th, 1853. Its object is to collect and preserve, and to open to the public, historical matter of all kinds, more especially that relating to Iowa, a general library, maps, charts, drawings, pictures, statuary, and a cabinet of natural history, also—to sustain public lectures. When the cabinet and library were destroyed by fire, the Institute was in a flourishing condition, having about 800 volumes in the library, 2000 pamphlets, files of newspapers since the organization of the Territory and State, and a great many papers pertaining to the early history and settlement of the State, about 4000 specimens illustrative of the geology of this State, an herbarium containing the greater portion of the plants found in the State, also a number of specimens illustrative of the zoology of the State; and a large collection of Indian relics, numbering about 400, among which were included nearly all the paraphernalia of Black Hawk. The loss sustained was irreparable, and for some time it was difficult to keep the Institute alive. For the last year, the Institute has been in a very flourishing condition;

in fact, so much so that a thorough re-organization was necessary. The present officers are—

"*President*, DAVID RORER.
Vice-President, WILLIAM THOMPSON.
Corresponding Secretary, JOHN H. RAUCH
Recording Secretary, A. D. GREEN.
Treasurer, LUKE PALMER.
Librarian, C. C. CLOUTMAN."

DUBUQUE COUNTY.

Dubuque is one of the oldest counties in the State, being one of the two original Districts, from which the principal eastern counties of the State were formed. It embraces the most noted portions of the mineral region, and, singular as it may appear, though in the very heart of the mineral region, the soil is generally of the most productive character, yielding large crops of grain. Few countries in the world possess the combined advantages of a soil rich in fertility, and at the same time underlaid with inexhaustible veins of lead ore. Lead is the great staple of export, as will be seen by the annexed statistics. Copper and zinc have also been discovered, but not in sufficient quantities to induce capitalists to enlist in the work of developing them. Several valuable lodes or veins of lead were discovered during the past winter.

The country west of Dubuque City is strikingly beautiful, and well watered. It is a rolling prairie, interspersed with groves of timber, while along the small streams run ning from north to south there are large bodies of good timber, and extensive water-power. Several adjoining counties, as well as Dubuque, are well settled—the land all entered by actual settlers. Mineral lots are laid off in almost every conceivable shape, and contain about ten acres each.

The city of Dubuque, one of the largest and most densely populated in the State, is handsomely situated upon a natural terrace. The streets run parallel to each other, and owing to the peculiar soil at this location, are never muddy. This city is more compactly built, and contains a greater proportion of fine buildings than any other place in the State. Among these the Catholic Cathedral, court-house, and hotels stand prominent. The city is bounded on the west by a range of high cliffs, from which the prospect of the city and county is entrancingly beautiful.

Three daily newspapers are published in Dubuque: the "Express and Herald," the "Tribune," and the "Observer," each issuing, beside, a weekly edition. The "Northwestern Farmer" (monthly) was commenced January 1, 1856—$1 a year.

The population of Dubuque County, according to the census of 1854, was 16,513; and of the city, 10,000; in April, 1856, 14,000. The number of buildings erected in the city during 1855 was 471.

Of the society in Dubuque we need not remark farther than to state, that this population of 14,000 ably supports twelve churches, one female seminary, one college, seven select and common schools, twenty-four lawyers, and fourteen doctors.

This city being the present terminus of two important

railroads, has recently become a place of great commercial importance.

Good investments can be made by the establishment, at Dubuque, of manufactories of Red and White Lead, Lead Pipe, Shot, and Sheet Lead. Capitalists should investigate this matter.

From the following statistics, the reader may judge of the commercial importance of the City of Dubuque :—

	Total Tonnage.	Value.
Imports to Dubuque in 1855......	276,699 05	$11,266,845 18
" " 1854.....	97,633	4,933,208 65
Increase	179,057 05	$6,333,636 53
Exports from Dubuque in 1855...	24,237 15	$3,689,266 58
" " 1854...	11,736	1,573,408 30
Increase	12,501 13	$2,115,858 28
Lead exported in 1855..............	5,262	$631,440
Iron, Steel, and Nails exp. in 1855	2,400	384,000
Flour exported in 1855.............	2,640	216,000
Wheat exported in 1855............	1,620	81,000
Corn exported in 1855..............	150	1,500

We invite the reader's particular attention to the following comparative table of immigration, for the past two years :—

Crossed the Dubuque Ferry	*in* 1854.	*in* 1855.
Men, women, and children	38,400	38,400
Wagons	4,300	10,700
Carriages..	2,100	4,200
Cattle	9,518	14,210
Sheep	2,708	4,680
Hogs	6,630	16,124

The number of arrivals at the Hotels at this point, in 1855, were 85,045. The amount of the public domain sold at the Dubuque Land Office during the year, was: cash sales, 808,923 acres; located with Military Warrants, 801,440. Received at the United States Depository, Dubuque, during the year, $4,146,550. Total amount of Eastern exchange sold by banking houses, $9,212,000.

DELAWARE COUNTY

Was first settled in 1843. Present population of the county, 8000—that of Delhi, the county-seat, 600.

There is one newspaper just started in the county under the title of "Delhi Republican," with very fair prospects of success.

The number and condition of public and private schools compare favorably with those of other counties in the state, of the same population.

No manufactories, yet some in contemplation. The county and its towns are filling up rapidly with an industrious, enterprising, and wealthy population. Great inducements are held out to capitalists to erect manufactories of different kinds. There is an abundance of water-power 1½ miles from Delhi, and a large body of timber on the Maquoketa, thus affording ample opportunity for the erection of machinery, whether propelled by steam or water-power. This county is peculiarly adapted to wool-growing; and all that is wanted to make the citizens of Delaware a great manufacturing people, is to make their advantages known to Eastern capitalists.

Chair-making, cabinet-making, wagon, carriage and buggy making, woollen factories, in short, everything, except *distilling alcoholic liquors*, is needed in this vicinity.

This county is conveniently interspersed with groves of timber, and drained by the Maquoketa, Plumb, Elk, Bear, Buffalo, Buck, Little Turkey, and Honey Creeks, all of which afford some fine mill-sites.

The prairie is gently undulating, soil good, composed of a happy admixture of vegetable mould and sand, based upon a porous clay subsoil. We have an abundance of fine lime-stone, for building and fencing purposes.

Near Delhi we have excellent clay for the manufacturing of brick, of the best quality.

Within a few rods of this village plat, we have a fine sheet of pure "*soft water*," covering about 160 acres of land, containing small fish in abundance, and affording a fine opportunity for bathing during the hot months.

Taking Delaware County as a whole, it affords as fine a chance for the wealthy, enterprising immigrant, as any county in Northern Iowa.

DECATUR COUNTY.

The population of Decatur County is 6000. The several denominations, Presbyterians, Methodists, Baptists and Christians, have each organizations, and have meetings in turn in the Court House in Leon, which is a respectable-sized two-story brick building. No buildings for public worship yet erected. No newspaper in Decatur or any adjoining county. In the county are some twenty-five public schools, well conducted, supported principally by the school fund. In the county are three steam, saw, and grist mills, and two others in process of erection. Those who may wish to locate, will find in Decatur good openings for saw and grist mills, brick-makers, wheelwrights, cabinet-makers, wagon-makers, house-builders, blacksmiths, tinners, and shoemakers.

The northern part of the county is principally prairies, while the southern is supplied with a large and beautiful growth of timber. Though the county is more broken than many north and east of it, the soil is all susceptible of cultivation, and more than half the county heavily timbered.

Thompson's Fork of Grand River and tributaries spreads over the western part of the county, affording an abundance of clear, soft water, and plenty of timber, for all purposes. These streams are backed by extensive beds of lime and sand-stone, suitable for building purposes, and supply water sufficient to run flouring or saw-mills, the year through.

Along the banks of several of these streams thin veins of coal have been discovered, and it is thought that extensive beds would be found by proper search, but no labor has yet been expended upon them.

Leon, the county-seat, is situated two miles due east of the centre of the county, within half a mile of an extensive body of excellent timber. The town was located in 1853, present population 400. The last session of the Legislature changed the name of this town to "Leon;" the Post Office yet bears the original name, "South Independence."

Decatur is pleasantly situated on a high, rolling prairie, $2\frac{1}{2}$ miles west of the centre of the county, and 3 miles from Thompson's Fork of Grand River. Population between 200 and 300.

FAYETTE COUNTY

Is abundantly watered by the Turkey River, its north and south forks, tributaries, and numerous springs. The soil is admirably adapted for all agricultural purposes. The scenery along Turkey River and its north and south forks is beautiful, and timber abundant. The principal towns in the county are West Union, the county-seat, Gamble Grove, Illyria, Fayetteville, Auburn, Elgin, Leo, Lima, and Taylorsville, besides post-offices named Eldorado, Eden, Clermont, Douglas, Windsor, and Louisville.

The population of Fayette County, in the spring of 1854, was 5042. Present population about 8000. West Union, the principal town and county-seat, numbers 800.

This county is very rich in minerals. Stone coal is said to be very abundant. Lead has also been found in small parcels in various parts of the county. A species of red ochre is abundant here, from which paint is made with but little trouble. It has been used upon buildings, looks well and is durable.

In Fayette County there are several very large caves that have never been explored, and numerous curiosities that would well repay the Naturalist or Geologist to visit and examine them. Some of the heaviest timber in the

State is in this county. Its growth and prosperity may be judged from the fact that a county Agricultural Society has been organised, and is well sustained.

FRANKLIN COUNTY.

A most excellent county of land—surface gently undulating. A few gravelly knolls are found in this county. Timber is rather scarce, but scattered through the county in the best manner to make it available. The county-seat is not yet located, but commissioners have been appointed for this purpose, and it soon will be. The county was organized at the election in August, 1855. It is well watered by the Iowa and Cedar rivers and by the tributaries of the latter. Fine specimens of marble have been found; to what extent it exists is not known. Population about 300.

FRÉMONT COUNTY

Is the extreme south-western county of the State. The first settlement was at Sidney, the county-seat, where the first sale of lots was made June 30th, 1851. James H. Cowles was the first resident. The present population of the county-seat is 400—that of the county 4200.

Of public schools there are in the county some twenty, with ample room for improvement in a majority of them.

The Congregational, Methodist, Baptist, Christians, and Presbyterians, have each societies here.

Here are a carding-machine, and two grist-mills, one

steam saw-mill, and four water-power saw-mills, all doing an excellent business. More manufactories and mechanics are needed. A steam flouring-mill would do a first-rate business.

The surrounding country is well adapted to all kinds of agricultural pursuits, possessing a rich and productive soil, well supplied with water and timber, and rapidly settling up with worthy, industrious and intelligent people.

GUTHRIE COUNTY

Is not as large nor as old as many other counties of the State, but possesses advantages which, when developed, will place her in the advance. The soil of Guthrie is second to none in the State, for the farmer, grazier, and fruit-grower. The numerous streams of running water afford eligible and profitable sites for the erection of the much-needed manufactories, while the banks are big with inexhaustible quarries of lime, free-stone, and stone-coal, and in the northwest corner large quantities of iron ore have been discovered. The first settlements in the county were made in 1850, and the present population is 3000. The principal church denominations are Methodists, United Brethren, O. S. Baptists, and Friends, each of whom are making arrangements for the erection of church buildings for their respective denominations.

Two newspapers have been recently established in this county—the Guthrie County Sentinel, at Panora, the county-seat, and the Western Pioneer, at Guthrie Centre, eight miles from Panora. These two, we believe, are the only papers west of Fort Des Moines, except the Bugle and Chronotype at Council Bluffs.

Panora was settled in 1853; it now contains a population of 200. More saw-mills, a planing-mill, lath-machine, carding and fulling-mill, brick-makers, carpenters, masons, and plasterers, are all much needed in Guthrie.

CHAPTER XVII.

DESCRIPTION OF COUNTIES—CONTINUED.

HARDIN COUNTY

WAS first settled in 1851—present population, 2000. There is an abundance of timber, coal, red and white sandstone, fine white limestone: lead and iron ore have also been found along Jena river, but no investigations have been made, as yet, of the quality or extent. The towns are all new; and in each, the capitalist, mechanic or tradesman, will find a brisk business at paying rates. The soil is excellent, climate pure and healthy, and the inhabitants enterprising and intelligent. Population of Hardin City, 350; of Eldora, the county-seat, 200; of Rocksylvania, 150; of Pokeepsie, 100. The tide of immigration will tend strongly into Hardin, and great improvements be made, in 1856.

HARRISON COUNTY,

Situated on the Missouri River, is but sparsely settled, yet a good proportion of the land in the county being entered. This county is well watered by the Boyer River, the Little Sioux, and various smaller streams, tributary to these and the Missouri. Magnolia is the county-seat, beside which there is no other settlement of importance. For a description of the soil see the chapter on Western Iowa, or Pottawattamie County.

HENRY COUNTY.

Mount Pleasant, the county-seat, was laid out in the year 1836, by Presley Saunders; at that time the lands on which it was located were not in market, nor had it ever been surveyed, but the beauty of the location, taken in connection with the great abundance of superior building-stone, and the large body of timber that lay contiguous to the site, to say nothing of the never-failing springs of water that gush from the shores of the branch that runs through the suburbs of the town, induced the proprietor to believe that a town might be built up that would be a credit to the State. Nor in this has he been disappointed. This town now contains a population of about 1500 inhabitants, and is at present in a more prosperous condition, and is improving faster than at any former period.

The population of the county in February last, was 11,180. Beside the county-seat, there are other towns in the county of considerable size and importance. Salem, in the south-west part of the county, is a thriving young place, containing 875 souls. New London, on the eastern edge of the county has some 650 inhabitants. Trenton, in the northern portion, some 500; beside these are Winfield, Lowell, Hillsborough, Rome, East Grove P. O., Marshall P. O., Wayne P. O., &c., all in a thriving condition.

There are six church edifices in Mount Pleasant; Congregational, Presbyterian, Methodist, Christian, O. S. Baptist, and Missionary Baptist. Other towns and villages are proportionally well supplied with churches, all of which are well attended, and in a healthy condition. In point of morality and sobriety, the community of Mount Pleasant is unsurpassed in the State.

One newspaper, "The Iowa Observer," is well-conducted, and well-sustained. The number of magazines and newspapers taken at that P. O. indicate the intelligence and refinement of the people.

Mount Pleasant has been named and known heretofore, as the point possessing and offering greater educational advantages than any other place in the State, and she has yet no rival in this respect except Davenport. The "Iowa Wesleyan University," under the control of the M. E. Church, is a Collegiate Institute of the first grade, has 150 students, and is in full and successful operation under the management of Prof. James Harlan, with competant assistants. The "Mt. Pleasant High School and Female Academy," under the management of Prof. S. L. Howe, a teacher of acknowledged ability and experience has an average attendance of 100 pupils. The well-merited reputation of this school at home and abroad is attested by the patronage it receives. A Select School for Young Ladies, under the superintendance of Rev. B. Wall, and taught by Mrs. Wall and Miss McHarg, has recently been opened, which bids fair to become a Female Seminary of usefulness and extensive patronage. The town and county is well supplied with well-attended and ably-conducted common schools.

There are at present no manufactories of importance in Henry County. Steam flouring and saw-mills, a foundry, and a carding and fulling-mill are much needed, and would prove good investments. Coal, in considerable quantities, has been found on both sides of the Skunk river, also inexhaustible quarries of the very best building stone near Mt. Pleasant. The Burlington and Missouri railroad will be finished to Mt. Pleasant during the present year. The Muscatine and Keokuk railroad also passes through Mt. Pleasant.

At the late session of the Legislature, the Iowa Insane Asylum was located at Mt. Pleasant, and fifty thousand dollars appropriated for the erection of the building.

The soil of Henry is second in quality to that of no other county in the State. The land is well watered, all entered, and rapidly filling up with a highly intellectual and industrious class of citizens.

IOWA COUNTY,

North of Keokuk, and west of Johnson, is well supplied with timber along the Iowa River, which stream, with the north fork of English River, Old Man's Creek, Beaver and Richmond Creeks, affords an abundance of water for all purposes. The soil is admirably adapted for farming and grazing. The county seat, Marengo, is situated upon the Iowa River, in the northern part of the county. There are settlements at Kozta, Homestead, Downard, Millersburg and North English Post Offices. The Mississippi and Missouri railroad passes through almost the centre of the county.

JACKSON COUNTY

Comprises in area fourteen full and six fractional townships of land. The principal towns in the county are Andrew, Bellevue, Wickliffe, Fulton, Maquoketa, Bridgeport, and some seventeen P. O. settlements beside.

During the past year great improvements have been made in Maquoketa and Bellevue, and mechanics and business men of all classes will here find good openings. The prospect of a Railroad connection with the East, at Lyons, has given Maquoketa a new impetus, and it is rapidly assuming the appearance of a city. At Bellevue, numerous mills, stores, warehouses, and dwellings are under contract to be erected this year—also the grading and paving of their levee.

Flouring and saw-mills are in active and profitable operation in different parts of the county, but it is impossible to obtain from their proprietors even an approximate esti mate of their profits.

At Bellevue, are excellent openings and good sites for two more steam saw-mills and a planing-mill. Lumber for building finds very ready sale as fast as manufactured, and lumber for sawing is easily obtained. A small iron foundry, an extensive wagon-making establishment, and a cooper's establishment, would all do well in Jackson.

Jackson is one of the best watered counties in the State, and is well supplied with timber, principally white oak, black walnut, ash, hickory, elm, maple, white walnut, and bass-wood. Water-power, unsurpassed for manufacturing purposes: upon several of the streams are already erected flouring and saw-mills, and others are in progress of erection. The county is also one of the best for agricultural purposes,in the State, and second to none for stock raising.

The soil in the valleys is a first rate black sandy loam (several feet in depth), and yields heavy crops of corn; the ridges are generally second and third rate soil, with a subsoil of clay, or in some instances ferruginous sand, and produce fine crops of wheat. Potatoes and other root crops, as well as vegetables and vines, all flourish luxuriantly. The rocks of the county are what belong to the "Upper Magnesian Limestone" formation; are well adapted for building purposes, and make a superior quality of lime.

Iron ore is found in various parts of the county, lying loosely on the surface, and no doubt, from present indications, it exists in large masses. "Galena" (lead ore) is also frequently picked up in different parts of the county, and some mines have been successfully worked in the northwest part of the county—there is a rich "lode" of "Galena" only three miles above Bellevue, dipping into the river, which can be seen at any time at a low stage of water in the Mississippi. It is the opinion of old miners, that when the mineral resources of this county are properly developed, it will prove rich in both lead and iron ores, as indications of its existence manifest themselves in almost every hill and ravine.

Bellevue, the seat of justice of Jackson county, is situated on the Mississippi river, twelve miles due south of the city of Galena; the town site is upon an elevated plateau of land about fifteen feet above high water mark; it is surrounded by an amphitheatre of hills, mostly covered with timber, which break off the severe cold winds of winter, and prevent the temperature from falling as low by several degrees, as a few miles distant upon the ridges.

The population of Bellevue is about 1200. The population of the county is fully 15,000; of Maquoketa, 1000, and emigrants daily arriving in every part of the county.

There are five organized churches in the town, viz., Congregationalist, Episcopalian, Methodist, Baptist, and Catholic—one of each.

JEFFERSON COUNTY.

The first sale of town lots took place in 1839.

The present population of Jefferson County is about 16,000. Population of Fairfield, the county-seat, 1600.

A large proportion of the population is from Ohio and Pennsylvania. In the eastern portion of the county is a settlement of Swedes, consisting at present of about 100 families. Their first settlement in that part of the county was made in 1847.

There is also in the north-east a settlement of Germans.

In Fairfield there are three churches: Presbyterian, Congregational, and Methodist.

Two newspapers in Fairfield; the "Fairfield Ledger," (Whig), and the "Iowa Sentinel," (Democrat).

Jefferson County contains 88 schools, and 65 school-houses, 59 of which are frame, the remaining 6 brick. Total amount paid teachers during the year, ending Oct. 31, 1854, $5,538 12. The average compensation of male teachers for the same time, was $20 35—that of females, $9 97! Number of pupils in schools, 3622.

A branch of the State University is located at Fairfield. A commodious building has been erected for the accommodation of pupils; and purchased by an association of citizens, who have established a flourishing school for young men and boys, under the charge of Mr. Anderson, a teacher of experience and ability.

There is also a Female Seminary in this place, which is in a prosperous condition, conducted by Rev. L. B. Crittenden.

Of manufactories the principal are a steam saw-mill, an iron foundery, a sash and door factory, and numerous minor establishments. We need a steam flouring-mill.

A United States Land Office, located in this place, has been closed, and business transferred to Chariton.

There are several thriving villages located in the different sections of the county, among which are Libertyville, seven miles south-west from Fairfield; Brookville and Abingdon, the former six, and the latter twelve miles west;

Pleasant Plain, twelve miles north; and Glasgow in the southern part of the county.

There are three extensive nurseries in the county. A county agricultural society was organized three years ago.

The "Iowa Farmer," an ably-conducted, well-supported, dollar, monthly agricultural paper, has been removed and permanently established at Fairfield.

The eastern part is well timbered. On the borders of Skunk River and its tributaries, are fine groves of various kinds of timber, suitable for building and fencing purposes. The most common are the white and burr oak, walnut, elm, cottonwood, and linn; sugar maple is found in some places on Skunk River. The western portion of the county is principally prairie, interspersed with some groves of timber, and is well adapted to cultivation, as no portion of that land is too broken, and none too flat, for cultivation.

Farms in the hands of residents are beginning to assume all the appearances of extensive and tasteful cultivation.

There are extensive beds of coal in different sections of the county. Also lime-stone is found along the borders of some creeks.

JOHNSON COUNTY.

Iowa City is the county-seat of Johnson County, and until the last session of the legislature, was the capital of the State. At that session a bill was passed, removing the seat of government to Fort Des Moines, in Polk County, some hundred and twenty miles further west; and providing for the erection of temporary public buildings, to be approved by the governor, before a session of the General Assembly will be holden there.

The present State House is not entirely finished, but is an elegant edifice of stone; capacious, well adapted to legislative and other public purposes, and an ornament to the city. This building, with its extensive grounds, is a grant to the State University, and will be appropriated to its use immediately upon the removal of the State offices and legislative sessions.

The University has an ample fund, and is now in operation in this city; well provided with competent professors, and temporarily occupying what is known as the Mechanics' Academy. The number of students is at present but about forty, as the first session was opened only on the first Monday of March, 1855.

Besides this infant institution, strong in resources and promises, there is the Female Collegiate Institute, in successful operation. This institution has been reared to its present prosperity, principally under the auspices of the Independent Order of Odd Fellows, in this city, and other portions of the State. The building designed for this seminary, will be completed, probably, during the present year, and no expense will be spared to render it equal in architectural beauty and finish to any in Iowa.

There is, also, the City Union School, with a principal and three assistants, besides numerous private schools, all thriving finely. There is no town in the State better supplied with educational advantages, considering its population.

A steam grist-mill is now operating successfully in this city; amount of business not known, as it has just commenced operations. Another is to be erected on the west side of the Iowa River the present season. About three miles west of town, or north-west, are Clarke's flouring-mills, clearing their owners at least $10,000 per annum.

The city is well stocked with churches, there being no less than seven church edifices, and eight religious societies. Of these, there are one Baptist, built of brick in superior style; an Old School Presbyterian, Methodist,—Protestant Methodist, Catholic, and Universalist, also of brick, and very creditable structures; and the New School Presbyterian, a neat stone edifice. The Episcopal Society worships in the basement of the Methodist Church.

According to the census of 1854, the population of the city was 3083; which is probably nearer six, than three thousand at the present time. It is situated at the junction of two great railroad routes—the one from Davenport, which has been running into the city since January 1, 1856, and the one from Clinton, which is being pushed forward with all possible dispatch. In no other place in the State will the change be greater or more favorable than in Iowa City, during the present year. Already have her weekly papers changed to tri-weekly; immense manufactories, mills, machine-shops, hotels, and large brick blocks of private and public buildings, are springing up as if by magic. Who can predict the future of this great railroad-centre, of the most fertile and most prosperous State in the Union?

(See Chapter on *Railroads*, and *Table of Post Offices*, for particulars on these subjects.)

The county is one of the finest agricultural counties in the State—well adapted for stock raising; also wheat, corn, and potatoes. A flourishing Agricultural Society of two years' standing is organized, and an immense interest is awakened in its behalf. The population at the last census was 8446, which is increasing at an astonishing rate.

JASPER COUNTY

Is bounded on the east by Poweshiek, west by Polk, north by Marshall, and south by Marion and a portion of Mahaska Counties. In no county in the State, perhaps, is there better soil for all purposes than in Jasper.

Probably no portion of our State surpasses Central Iowa in point of beauty, fertility, healthfulness of climate, and the thriftiness of its inhabitants.

In 1846, the Senatorial Legislature formed it out of a portion of Mahaska County; and, in 1847, Newton, the county-seat of Jasper, was laid out by Thomas Henderson and Jacob Fisher.

Large quantities of fine stone-coal are found in the immediate vicinity of the place, and the traveller often finds it upon the surface of the ground. When we consider that this article seems almost inexhaustible, there can scarcely be a question as to the profitableness of almost any branch of mechanical and manufacturing industry which may be established in this portion of our State. Lime-stone, suitable for building purposes, is found on the banks of Elk Creek and Skunk River; this one article greatly facilitates the operations of our citizens in erecting buildings, and in many other ways. One grist-mill and two saw-mills are now in successful operation; but the demand for mills is constantly increasing. Men of capital, and true Western spirit, are making arrangements to erect forges and workshops, which, when completed, will render Newton quite a point for manufacturing. Mr. William P. Cole is working a coal bank, which has a strata of good coal 5 feet thick, and of an extent unknown—situated on South Skunk, Sec. 32, T. 80, R. 21.

The M. and M. R. R., already built to Iowa City, is rapidly extending her iron arms westward, and will soon place Newton upon the great Iron Highway to the Atlantic.

The present population of Jasper County is about 8000; of Newton, 750; of Monroe, 200; of Quincy, 200.

JONES COUNTY

Was first settled in 1836, organized in 1839, and the county-seat located at Anamosa in May, 1847. The population of the county in October, 1854, was 6300—being about eleven to the square mile. In this county will be found a due proportion of timber land and prairie land; while the mill-sites upon the Wabsipinnicon are numerous, and building-stone abundant. Beside the Wapsie', are the North and South Forks of the Maquoketa, Bear, and Mineral Creeks, and numerous first-rate springs of good water. The towns in the county are Anamosa, Rome, Bowen's Prairie, Fairview, and Monticello. In Anamosa is published one newspaper, "The News." There are also one Congregational and one United Brethren church edifices, and organizations each, of Methodists, Christians, and Universalists. The Masons and Odd Fellows each have Lodges there. The Iowa Central Air-Line Railroad passes through the county, touching at Anamosa. This line is located and under contract as far as Marion, Linn County.

CHAPTER XVIII.

DESCRIPTION OF COUNTIES—CONTINUED.

KEOKUK COUNTY

Is the third county from the Mississippi River and the Missouri State-line; situated west of Washington, and north-west of Jefferson Counties. The land is of an excellent quality, well watered by the Checauque and its tributaries, which are skirted with a good supply of timber. Lancaster, the county-seat, has increased very rapidly during the past two years, as has the entire county.

The Muscatine and Oskaloosa Railroad, which is under contract, passes through the county, touching the county-seat. Sigourney, Waugh's Point, and Richland are each centres of large settlements of intelligent and industrious people; the latter place is settled principally by Friends, or Quakers.

KOSSUTH COUNTY.

This is the second county in extent in the State, comprising what was formerly Bancroft, Kossuth, and the north part of Humboldt. It contains eight hundred and twenty-nine thousand four hundred and forty acres. Its population is about 300. Some of the northern townships are rather sloughy; but the county generally has as fine lands as are found in the State. The East Branch of the Des Moines River passes through this county near its centre, east and west, for a distance of fifty miles. There are fine groves of timber nearly the whole extent. The county was organized in August, 1855, although the lands are not in market, and Asa C. Call, the first settler, elected County Judge. One saw-mill is already erected. This county affords some of the best chances of any in the State. Its settlers are of the most enterprising class. Alquona is the county-seat, and is situated on the east bank of the east fork of the Des Moines River. Three or four towns have been laid out in this county, but we cannot give the location of them, nor the name of but one, Cresco; the place to be built up by the Western Home Association, of which H. Kellogg, of Cleveland, Ohio, is President.

LEE COUNTY

Is situated at the junction of the Mississippi and the Des Moines Rivers, and is the most southern county in the state; it is bounded on the south-east by the Mississippi, which separates it from Illinois; on the south-west by the Des Moines, separating it from Missouri; on the west by Van Buren; and on the north by Henry and Des Moines Counties. The county is well watered by the Des Moines and Mississippi and their tributaries. The principal towns are Keokuk, Montrose, Fort Madison, West Point, Franklin, Nashville, &c.

The bottom-lands of Lee are well adapted to the wants of the agriculturist, and its prairies are elevated, dry and rolling. The business of stock-raising has been entered into in Lee more extensively perhaps than in any other county.

The city of Keokuk, the largest place in the county, is situated at the foot of the Des Moines or Lower Rapids, at the extreme south-east corner of the state. By the usual routes of travel it is 230 miles from Chicago; 210 from St. Louis; 400 from the junction of the Ohio and Mississippi; 1000 from New York; and 1400 from New Orleans. Its position as a central commercial point is scarcely equalled by that of any other city west of Chicago, and endows it with business advantages and facilities of the highest importance. These advantages are three-fold, and may be treated of under the three following heads, viz:—

First, those derived from the navigation of the Mississippi. The Lower Rapids, formed by a rocky stratum in the river, commencing about 200 yards above the city, and running northward a distance of 12 miles, with a fall of 24 feet, render Keokuk the head of navigation during a great portion of the year, until the work of improving the Rapids is completed. At present, in time of low water, steamers are obliged to unload their cargoes into "lighters," which are towed up the Rapids, above which the freight is again loaded into the boats; and thus this city is rendered a wholesale depôt, and place of transhipment.

The *second* point lies in the trade of the Des Moines Valley which Keokuk must inevitably command, situated but 2 miles above the confluence of the Des Moines and Mississippi Rivers. This valley, for a width of sixty miles on either side of the Des Moines River, is unsurpassed probably in the world for agricultural wealth. It also abounds in timber, coal, gypsum, and many other articles of trade, and these will be transmitted down the Des Moines to its mouth at Keokuk, thence re-shipped to other markets. Of the improvement of the Des Moines we speak at length in another Chapter.

The *third* source of business advantages which Keokuk can claim, lies in its railroads. The Keokuk and Fort Des Moines, the Keokuk, Mt. Pleasant and Muscatine, and the Eastern railroads will soon be built, and will afford this city numerous connections of the highest importance.

Keokuk is situated upon a bluff 150 feet above high-water mark in the Mississippi, is laid out one mile square, and contains a population of about 10,000. Its streets are wide and regular, and are being graded and McAdamized with rapidity. Main Street, 100 feet in width, is McAdamized through the city for a distance of one mile. The city contains six brick-yards, two lumber-yards, one flouring and grist-mill, two foundries, one machine shop, five hotels, &c.

Its public school is held in the largest and handsomest building, which, throughout the State, is devoted to the cause of education. The edifice, when fully completed, will have cost $13,500. This city also contains the Iowa Medical College, a State institution, and a Female Seminary, besides two other female institutes, and a number of private schools. Six church edifices, O. and N. S. Presbyterian, Baptist, Methodist, Episcopalian and Catholic. See chapters on "Railroads," and "Public Improvements."

The bluff on which the city stands contains the finest of lime-stone, for building and other purposes, and commands a landscape view of wild and picturesque beauty.

LINN COUNTY

Is the third from the Mississippi River, and in the very heart of a rich agricultural region. The county is well supplied with water, and extensive water-power, by the Red Cedar and Waubsepinnicon Rivers, and Buffalo Creek, each of which pass through it, and the banks of which are heavily timbered. Present population, 13,000.

Cedar Rapids, the largest town in the county, is built upon both sides of the Cedar River—has an immense water-power, (as its name indicates), and is the agricultural, commercial, and manufacturing centre and mart, of not only Linn, but several surrounding counties. The Chicago, Iowa and Nebraska Railroad is under contract, being rapidly pushed forward, and it is believed will be completed from Clinton to Cedar Rapids early next year, thus connecting

Cedar Rapids and Linn County with the East. Present population of Cedar Rapids, 2300.

Marion, the county-seat, is situated five miles north-east from the Rapids, surrounded on the east, west, and south by fine groves of timber, adjoining which are farms under the highest state of cultivation. This town is beautifully located, and its citizens exhibit much good judgment as well as good taste, in the erection of substantial and beautiful buildings, for business and for residences. Attention is also paid to adorning and cultivating their grounds and parks which would be creditable to larger towns. Some idea may be formed of the business of Marion, from the fact that eleven extensive dry-goods stores are each doing a lucrative business.

Of educational edifices and institutions, there are at Cedar Rapids, two female seminaries, one high school, and several schools for less advanced pupils. Efforts are being made for the establishment of a college, also. Marion supports several ably-conducted schools, and has one of the best buildings for common-school purposes, in the State. These, with her court-house, five churches, and the large, tasteful blocks of buildings, give Marion a prepossessing appearance.

The "Iowa Conference Seminary," is located at Mount Vernon—has a brick edifice 40 by 72 feet, 3 stories high. It is in a very prosperous condition, under the superintendence of Rev. S. M. Fellows, A. M., assisted by three regular teachers, besides music teacher, and teacher of painting and embroidery. Number of students now in attendance about 150; most of them young ladies and gentlemen from abroad. The situation is unsurpassed for beauty.

The Iowa Central Air-Line Railroad is under contract to Marion, to which point the company expect to have the road graded this season.

Present population of Marion, 1800.

Those wishing particular information of, or having business to transact in Linn, will be well served by Messrs. Dodge & Wood, bankers, collectors, and general land agents, Cedar Rapids.

The Cedar Valley Times, Cedar Valley Farmer, and the Linn County Register, (the latter at Marion), are well patronized and worthy papers.

LOUISA COUNTY

Is bounded by the Mississippi on the east, which, with the Iowa and Cedar Rivers, traversing it diagonally through the centre, present an abundance of water and timber.

The present population of the county is 8700, and of Wapello, the county-seat, 1200.

The railroad from Muscatine to Oskaloosa, is in a fair way to be completed early this year, and, passing through this county, will do much to make known the undeveloped resources and "hidden treasures" of this region.

This county embraces a principal portion of the Keokuk Reserve, purchased by the Government in 1836. It is a remarkable fact, that almost the whole tribe of Sacs and Foxes were congregated *here* until after the first or Black Hawk purchase of 1832; notwithstanding they had almost a boundless region from which to select their villages and hunting-grounds.

Wapello, the seat of justice, is handsomely located on the old site of "Wapello's Village." Wapello was a Fox chief, who resided there until the summer of 1836, as chief of his band. There are several small villages in Louisa, among which are Toolsboro', Columbus City, Harrison, Florence, Fredonia, &c. Toolsboro'—formerly Black Hawk —is situated upon the north side of the Iowa, about three miles from the Mississippi, has an extensive country trade, and is somewhat celebrated for its ancient mounds and fortifications.

Florence derives its principal notoriety from its having been the residence of Black Hawk until the Indian hostilities in 1832. Here repose the bones of his ancestors, where they have rested for centuries. It was here that he sounded the war-whoop, and rallied his countrymen to the last deadly conflict, in defence of the homes and the graves

> "Where sleep their warriors; where rival chieftains lay,
> And mighty tribes, swept from the face of day."

But they were conquered, and this illustrious warrior was doomed to wander, a stranger in the land of his forefathers. His lodge was still standing at the time the country was surveyed.

MADISON COUNTY,

Recently organized, is but sparsely settled. The soil is good, climate healthy, and land very cheap. Population of county, 4500—of Wintusett, county-seat, 700.

MAHASKA COUNTY,

Of which Oskaloosa is the county-seat, is a thriving and populous county for its age. The first settlements in the county were made in 1842, on the public land, and in June, 1843, the county-seat was organized by commissioners appointed by the Legislature. The present population of Oskaloosa is nearly 3500.

The advantages this county boasts, are her central position in the State; her universally fertile soil, (producing an average of 80 bushels of corn to the acre); the abundance of water, and extensive water-power furnished by the Des Moines, North and South Skunk, and their tributaries; her inexhaustible quarries of free, lime, and sand stone; her extensive and variously distributed beds of stone coal; her bounteous supply of timber along each water-course that traverses the county; and the industry, intelligence, and high moral tone and character of her inhabitants.

Oskaloosa, being the county-seat and commercial centre of this rich agricultural district, is an important town. It is well supplied with grist and saw-mills, machine-shops, and manufactories of different kinds. Four hotels are doing a good business, and another, 120 feet front on two streets, is about to be built. Two ably-conducted and well-sustained newspapers, (the Times, democratic, and the Herald, republican), are published in Oskaloosa, and a third is about to be established.

MARION COUNTY

Was settled in October, 1845, by Wilson Stanley, L. G. Terry, L. W. Babbitt, Dr. R. Mathews, E. & T. Jenkins, J. D. Bedell, and E. G. Stanfield. The present population of the county is 14,000—of Knoxville, the county-seat, 1100.

In the county-seat are one Methodist, and one Congregational, edifices. The different denominations are Methodist, Lutheran, Congregational, Presbyterian, Baptist, Missionary Baptist, Associate Reformed, and United Brethren.

The number of public schools is stated to be sixty-six. Two high schools—one in Knoxville, another in Pella—all in a prosperous condition. A college is being erected in Pella by the Missionary Baptists.

Several steam saw and flouring-mills in operation, but threefold more needed. Also manufactories of all kinds wanted.

Soil good for farming purposes, timber plenty, water abundant and excellent. Prairie unsurpassed by any in the Union. Climate good. Winters admirably adapted for stock, owing to their dryness and evenness. Stone-coal, of excellent quality, abounds in veins eight feet thick. Splendid lime and sandstone, for building purposes, abundant.

Knoxville, and Pella, are each thrifty, active, business places. Pella was laid out in 1848, by Henry P. Schotte, of Holland. It contains now about 1500 inhabitants, principally Hollanders. They are a steady, industrious, honest class of people, and brought considerable wealth with them.

Two steam saw-mills, sash and door factory, plow factory, a patent brick, and a carding machine, also an oil-mill, are all in course of construction, at Pella. Mechanics and builders, manufacturers and capitalists, are needed at both Pella and Knoxville. One German, and two American schools, in successful operation at Pella.

Persons wanting information of this county, can refer to Schotte & Grant, bankers and land agents, also publishers of the "Pella Gazette," and of the "Bankers' and Land Agents' Monthly Bulletin;" or to Brobst & Miller, surveyors and land agents, Knoxville. (See list of *Post Offices*, another chapter.)

MARSHALL COUNTY

Though new, is improving rapidly. Population in 1854, 1703—in 1855, 2500—in February, 1856, 3600—of Marietta, county-seat, 200. The Iowa River and tributaries, traversing the county, are well-timbered. Lead, iron, limestone, and free-stone, in considerable quantities, exist in this county.

MILLS COUNTY.

Glenwood, the county-seat, was first settled by the Mormons, in 1847, and this was about the first settlement in the county; but that population has long since been almost entirely supplanted by people from Michigan, New York, Ohio, and Missouri.

The present population of the town is about eight hundred—that of the county about six thousand.

For description of soil and climate, see chapter on Western Iowa and Nebraska.

There are three churches in the place, viz.: Methodist, Congregationalist, and Presbyterian (Old School); in the county, ten churches, belonging to the same denominations.

Two newspapers are published in the county: the "Glenwood Times," and the "St. Mary's Gazette."

There are a large Union School and two District Schools in the town, and about twenty common schools in the county, all in a flourishing condition, and supplied with good teachers. There is still a great demand for teachers.

They have one flouring and two saw-mills — the two latter driven by steam. There are fifteen mills in the county, one carding-machine, and a shingle-mill. All of the above named are overstocked with business, and there is abundance of room for others. Cabinet-makers, weavers, cloth-fullers, tanners, house-builders, and every class of mechanics, are much needed.

MITCHELL COUNTY

Is in the northern tier of counties, and although new, is fast filling up with actual settlers. The town of Osage is the principal settlement now in the county, and has a population of 800. One of the proprietors authorizes us to say, that they will give a lot to every mechanic who will permanently locate there—until the town has 2000 inhabitants. [Most of the smaller interior towns throughout the State will do the same.] A steam-mill, and a portable grist-mill, are among the improvements. There is a report in circulation at the present writing, (March 1, 1856), that the Land Office for the Turkey River District, will be removed to Osage, this Spring.

MONONA COUNTY

Is the central one, of those bordering upon the Missouri River; it is well watered by the Little Sioux and Soldier Rivers, and numerous lakes, and is well-timbered. This and the adjoining counties have considerable unentered land, which actual settlers would do well to locate upon. Ashton is the county-seat. The Iowa Central Air-Line Railroad is projected to reach the Missouri, in this county.

MONROE COUNTY

Was organized in 1843, and the county-seat "laid off" in 1844. Present population of the county, 4200—of Albia, the county-seat, 400.

Steam flouring-mills, saw-mills, coopering establishments, cabinet-ware manufactories, and any number of industrious mechanics are greatly needed here. At present the cooperage for pork, lard and flour, is obtained from a great distance, at decided disadvantage.

This county is as well watered as any portion of the State. The principal streams which have their rise in, or pass through the county, are Cedar Creek, Whippoorwill Creek, White's Creek, and Coal Creek; the three latter, with numerous smaller streams, emptying into Cedar Creek, render it of proper size and power for mill-sites, and there are now five mills erected on this stream, doing business more than half the year. Bluff's, Gray's, Miller's, Avery's, and Soap Creeks, are each streams of some size, and skirted with timber averaging nearly a mile in width.

Throughout the county the soil is very good; the prairies are small, high, and fertile. An abundance of timber, coal, and limestone may be found in most parts of the county. The best land is entered, but claims to some of the very best can be bought at from five to ten dollars per acre. The county is increasing in numbers very rapidly, and offers great inducements to manufacturers, mechanics, farmers, and citizens of all classes.

MUSCATINE COUNTY.

[NOTE.—Inasmuch as the greatest (and so far as we can learn, *only*) opposition urged against the circulation of the first edition of this work, was from the press of Muscatine, who claim that the population and importance of their city was underrated, the author prefers, in the present volume, to give the exact statements furnished by two of the most intelligent, deeply interested, and wealthy men of the city:

Population of Muscatine, 7,568.

Schools—two public, and two select.

Manufactories in operation.—Carriage and wagon, 7; boot and shoe, 12; cooperage, 7; cabinet-ware, 10; bedstead, 1; chair, 1; sash and blind, 3; foundery and machine, (small) 1; flour-mills, 3; saw-mills, 2; stave and shingle, 2 each.

Manufactories needed.—A large foundery and machine shop, for boilers, engines, &c.; a manufactory for reapers,

Concretions in Carboniferous Sandstone, Muscatine.

and farming implements generally; for wagons, carriages, and furniture.

Proof.—During the past year four of the forwarding houses have received from the East—

Engines	24	Separators	18
" portable	6	Corn and Cob Mills	24
Boilers, large	27	Wagons, large	391
Reapers and Thrashers	206	Carriages and Buggies	65

Also needed.—1st. One or more good, efficient newspapers, with material for good job-work; good printers, with capital to establish themselves in business; 2d, a good academy, or high school, for both sexes—in this we are wofully deficient, and a better opening is not to be found in the State; 3d, a good bookbinder—one can do well, and have a clear field.

Mechanics and business men needed.—School-teachers of a superior character; foundrymen, machinists, chair-makers, (an immense number of chairs are landed here for the interior.)]

This county is situated next below Scott County, on the Mississippi River, and contains an area of 432 square miles. The name of this county was derived from a tribe of Indians known as the Muscoutins.

The city of Muscatine is located upon uncommonly broken ground, and a majority of the lots, either for business or residences, require grading; the citizens, however, are of that class, who, appreciating the superiority of their location in other respects, have by art made smooth Nature's rough places, and tasteful and stately residences now grace bluffs, wnich, but a few months ago, were almost inaccessible.

Two newspapers are published in Muscatine: a Whig, weekly and tri-weekly; and a Democratic, weekly.

The inhabitants have the character of being second to none in the State in point of intelligence and industry.

CHAPTER XIX.

DESCRIPTION OF COUNTIES—CONTINUED.

PAGE COUNTY,

Situated on the Missouri line, and within one county of the Missouri River, is of good arable land, well watered, well timbered, and but sparsely settled, the largest town in the county is the county-seat. Actual settlers will here find locations to suit them, at their own prices. There is yet some vacant land in this, and the adjoining county.

PALO ALTO COUNTY

Contains much very excellent land, mainly Prairie. Along the Des Moines River, which passes diagonally through it, scattering bodies of timber are found. Near the centre is Medium Lake, which is about seven miles in length and one in width. A few pioneers are settled in this county.

POCHAHONTAS COUNTY

Is composed of prairie almost entirely. The West Fork of the Des Moines River passes through its easterly boundary, and it is pretty well watered by its tributaries. There are yet no settlers in this county.

POLK COUNTY

Was opened for settlement in May, 1846. The garrison was removed in July of that year, and in the same month and year, the town of Fort Des Moines was laid out.

The population of Polk County is upwards of 8000; that of Fort Des Moines, 1900.

In the county are Episcopal, Presbyterian (Old and New School), Baptist, Methodist, and Catholic churches—the latter but recently established.

Business of all kinds has increased more rapidly during the past year than ever before.

Two private schools and one public school in Fort Des Moines; the former in good condition, affording a respectable academic course for young ladies and gentlemen. A large District school-house, on the "Union" plan, is in course of erection, to be completed this fall, costing some $6000.

The Des Moines River passes diagonally through Polk County, entering at the north-west and passing out at the south-east corner. Raccoon River empties into this river at Fort Des Moines. Both of these streams afford numerous sites for manufactories and mills. There are several grist and saw-mills in the county, but not a tithe of the number that are needed. Our correspondent writes: "We need more shops of all descriptions, and, above all, manufactories. We want flouring-mills and saw-mills—more of them, and on a larger scale. We want brick-makers, carpenters, cabinet-makers, brick and stone masons, plasterers, and, in short, mechanics of all kinds. We want water-wheels and steam-engines, farmers, machinists, and day-laborers."

Polk County, as well as those adjoining, and those farther north and west, is high, rolling prairie, with a due proportion of timber, and is well watered with rivers and creeks, the banks of which abound in coal, lime, sandstone, and gypsum in great quantities.

The last session of the Legislature located the Capital of the State at Fort Des Moines, since which time that place has been almost besieged by lawyers, doctors, agents, and land speculators.

Fort Des Moines is destined to be one of, if not *the*, largest interior city in the State. The Public Buildings of the State will probably soon be under contract, and the Railroad west from Iowa City is daily nearing this new capital. We anticipate an almost unprecedented advance in the wealth and population of Fort Des Moines during the present year.

POTTAWATAMIE COUNTY.

(See Chapter on *Western Iowa and Nebraska.*)

POWESHEIK COUNTY

Is composed principally of prairie soil, with but little timber except on its eastern, western, and northern borders. The county now contains a population of 3200. The Mississippi and Missouri Railroad passes through the centre of the county, and its completion will add much to the wealth, size, and importance of every town on the line, and to the county at large. Grinnell is on this railroad, and though but 18 months old, contains steam-mills and manufactories, and 300 inhabitants. The "People's College" of Iowa is located here, and funds are in the hands of the Trustees for the erection of the first building this year. The District school-house under contract here, will cost, completed, $5000.

RINGGOLD COUNTY

Is situated on the Missouri State line, has been recently organized and contains but about 800 inhabitants. The only organized town in the county is Mount Air, the county-seat, with a population of about 100 inhabitants. This county is densely timbered in some portions, and well watered. There is vacant land in this and the adjoining counties, to enter.

SAC COUNTY

Is an excellent county of land, well watered by the Coon and Boyer Rivers, and their tributaries. New Munich is a town recently laid out by Thomas Cavanaugh, Esq., 40 miles west of Fort Dodge, on the State road. This is a delightful prairie location, adjoining large bodies of timber.

A steam saw-mill and other machinery is being erected. This will be the county-seat. Mechanics and farmers, here is an open field for you.

SCOTT COUNTY

Is situated on the Mississippi (which bounds it on the east and south), and is the lower one of the trio which occupy a front and central rank among the counties bordering on the river. The first permanent settlement in the county was made by Antoine Le Claire, in the spring of 1833. During the next year several families and companies of whites crossed over as "squatters," settling upon such "claims" as might suit their fancy. Mr. Le Claire was for many years intimately and responsibly identified with our government in its intercourse with the Indians of the north-west, being in government service, as interpreter and Indian agent, from 1813 to 1843 — 30 years; and in some ten or twelve important treaties, he was the principal or only interpreter, and as such attended the government officers on the occasion. His familiarity with some fourteen Indian dialects, as well as with the English and French languages, and his being the great-grand-son of a chief, and his wife the descendant of another, gave him an influence with, and a knowledge of the Indian tribes, such as no other individual of his day possessed.

The marquee of Gen. Scott, in which was held the treaty with the Sac and Fox Indians, was erected upon the identical spot, which has, since 1833, been occupied by Mr. Le Claire as a residence. On the preceding page is

L'Eclaire's Homestead.

presented a view of the Le Claire Homestead, which was occupied as a residence by Mr. Le Claire from 1833 to 1854. In the spring of 1854 it was given up to the Mississippi and Missouri Railroad Company, as a location for their passenger depôt.

At the period of the treaty made by Gen. Scott, the cholera was prevailing among the soldiers in the Fort, and the meeting, instead of being held on the Island, was, from prudential considerations, transferred to the main shore, though not outside of the range of the guns of the Fort. It was in this marquee that the chief of the Sacs made a present of a mile square of land to Mrs. Le Claire, and, striking his foot upon the turf, told Mr. Le Claire that the only condition he asked was that he should build his house upon that spot—a condition that was speedily complied with.

The treaty was held in the fall of 1832, and ratified by Congress the following winter. In the spring of 1833, Mr. Le Claire erected a small building, or "shanty," in the then Fox village, "Morgan," which had occupied this ground for years previous. Of the tribe having this as their head-quarters, *Maquopom* was the head warrior, and *Poweshcik* head chief. In the fall of 1834, the Sac and Fox Indians left here for the Cedar River. In the spring of 1836 the town of Davenport was laid out under the supervision of Alexander W. McGregor, Esq., one of the first who camped and cabined here; and whose son, now 18 years of age, is the oldest native of Scott County. Additions have recently been made to the original plat, until the present city limits extend 3 miles along the river, and probably two in width.

Rock Island is about three miles in length, with an average width of half a mile, and contains therefore nearly one thousand acres. The rapids commence some twelve miles above it and terminate at its foot. Moline and the city of Rock Island, on the Illinois shore, are opposite its extreme endings, and the city of Davenport and East Davenport occupy nearly the same relation to it on the Iowa side. At the foot of the Island stands old Fort Armstrong, built in 1816, by Col. Mason, U. S. A. Half a mile distant, on the north side of the Island, is the residence of the late Col. Davenport, who was for more than 30 years a partner in the American Fur Company, and an Indian trader. On the 4th of July, 1845, a band of robbers entered his beautiful residence in the middle of the day, in the absence of his family, and in robbing him accidentally shot him; he died the same night. After having lived a frontier life for so many years, and having passed through a long and bloody Indian war, he was doomed to die by the hands of desperadoes. All the murderers were taken; three were hung at Rock Island, the same year—but two escaped, and are yet at large. From 1837 to '40, and up to '45, Iowa and northern Illinois were infested by the most daring set of outlaws that have ever visited the western world. But the supremacy of the laws has banished them from our midst, and Iowa is again comparatively free from crime.

The Island is now covered with a dense growth of young timber, of every variety, that flourishes in this climate. Forty years ago, Mr. Le Claire states, this ground was covered by a very dense forest, but the soldiers stationed in the Fort and the early settlers of the country, destroyed much of it for fuel and other purposes, and finally fire was communicated to the bed of leaves which had accumulated there for ages, and swept the Island of its crowning glory. The present growth of timber dates its origin subsequent to this fire.

"The Island, with the exception of a fractional quarter section of about one hundred and fifty-five acres, which was given to Col. Davenport, belongs to the government. The motives which led to withholding it from sale, so long as Fort Armstrong was occupied, and there remained a necessity of keeping an armed force in this vicinity, are evident enough. But the Fort was really abandoned in 1835, and the policy which has induced the government to retain its hold upon the Island since that period, is not so apparent. Numerous efforts have been made to obtain an order for its sale, and it is to be feared, in too many instances, with the view of securing the possession of it to a few favored individuals. Twice have such orders been issued by the proper departments, but on both occasions the sale was not permitted to proceed. Under the circumstances it was well that it did not. This magnificent body of land, lying here in the midst of so much beauty, and surrounded by towns which bid fair to become the seat of an immense commerce, should not be permitted to fall into the hands of mere speculators. But the Island should unquestionably pass from public to private ownership. As it is, it answers no useful end to the government or to individuals, and its being retained by the former retards in many ways the prosperity of the neighboring towns and country."

15*

Since the completion of the Chicago and Rock Island Railroad, Davenport has moved forward with rapid strides; and the extension of the M. & M. R. R. to Iowa City, has made this place an important commercial point. Along the line of this pioneer Iowa railroad, villages and towns have sprung up at the several depôt stations, each forming a nucleus for larger towns, and an outlet for the products of an extensive agricultural district. Of these we can give the names of Wolcott, Fulton, Duvant, Junction, and Moscow, on the Cedar River.

Le Claire, 13 miles above Davenport, is a thrifty town of 1600 inhabitants. Being at the head of the Upper Rapids, this place possesses an advantage over points below, as a lumber mart, and renders it, during the season of low water, a re-shipping point; goods being transported by wagons between Davenport and Le Claire, around the Rapids.

In Davenport, in 1854, there were 400 buildings erected; in 1855, 600, of a better class—larger and more substantial; and in 1860, the prospect is that at least 1000 more will be added to the present "Bridge City." During the past two years, six large and commodious church edifices have been erected and dedicated; mills, manufactories, and business blocks have been built which would be an honor to the largest commercial cities.

The following statistics will give some idea of the business transacted:—exported in 1855, barley, 60,000 bus.; wheat, 364,000; corn, 150,000; oats, 12,000; rye, 5,000; potatoes, 52,700; onions, 16,500. Hogs, 20,000. This account does not include the numerous droves of hogs and cattle, and the loads of grain and produce that daily cross the river, and are sent east by the Rock Island Railroad. Beside the lumber bought from rafts, and that brought from Chicago, there were 10,475,000 feet sawed and sold from the mills of this city. Capital invested in manufacturing, $700,000; in trade and merchandise, $1,000,000; in banking, $397,000. The four banking houses, beside their land business, have sold of exchange, $2,650,000; discounted and loaned, $1,240,000. The above figures apply to last year, 1855.

Of churches there are 1 Episcopal, 1 Presbyterian, (O. S.), 1 Congregational, 2 Baptist, 1 each, Methodist, Lutheran, and Disciples, and 2 Catholic Churches, and 16 clergymen.

Of educational institutions, the Iowa College, (Congregational), the Ladies' College, and the Public School edifices, are each (just being finished), large and commodious buildings, possessing all the modern improvements, and located upon sites commanding most extensive and picturesque landscape views.

We have devoted more space to the description of Scott County, the Island, &c., than to any other county in the State, but probably no more than they deserve. At no point in the whole Mississippi Valley is presented a more beautiful location for a city than here, and nowhere else in the West can be found two cities of the size of Rock Island and Davenport, opposite each other, together concentrating a population of nearly 25,000 inhabitants;—individually cities of great importance to the West—together forming one of the most attractive points on the Upper Mississippi.

The purlieus of these two cities have also been the scenes of a number of incidents, which tend to imbue with a deep and thrilling interest, the early history of Iowa. A relation of these would occupy a greater space than it is in our power at present to devote to them; but we are preparing to compile them, together with an accurate and compendious history of the primitive days of the entire State, for publication at an early period.

Since our chapter on Geology was completed, and in print, an extensive bed of *Cannel coal* has been penetrated, in Scott County, which promises to be of great value to its possessors. The area underlaid by this bank embraces several acres. Specimens of this coal which have been furnished us, burn well, are very light and brittle, and susceptible of a polish, though inferior to the Cannel coal of Pennsylvania. It is thought by colliers that the better qualities are farther in the banks. In our next edition we shall be able to give a chemical analysis of the properties of this coal.

SHELBY COUNTY,

Lying north of Pottawattamie, is well supplied with water, timber, and building materials. Most of the land in this county, and in those adjoining on the north and east, is to be entered at $1.25 per acre. For description of soil and climate see chapter on "*Western Iowa.*"

STORY COUNTY

Is a good body of prairie land, lying north of Polk, and between Boone and Marshall. Recently organized and sparsely settled.

CHAPTER XX.

DESCRIPTION OF COUNTIES—CONCLUDED.

TAMA COUNTY.

THE county-seat of Tama was but two years old last November. In February, 1856, it contained 200 inhabitants—the county upwards of 500. In 1850, the county contained but 8 inhabitants—5 males and 3 females—something of an increase!

Hydraulic privileges excellent in the county, on the Iowa River—also, an abundance of water-power on Deer, Wolfe, Honey, and Otter Creeks. We have 4 saw-mills—2 water, 2 steam. One flouring-mill, with two runs of stones.

Excellent opening for lumber, flour, or woollen manufactories, at Toledo and Indiantown.

Tama County is of rich, alluvial soil. The prairie and timber lands are exceedingly well proportioned to each other. Both upland and river-bottom timber in abundance for all the wants of the county, for fencing, building, and purposes of fuel. It is confidently asserted that there is an abundance of coal in the county, but no banks have as yet been opened.

The face of the county is greatly undulating, with a good proportion of river bottom, two to four miles in width —well watered. The soil yields wheat, hemp, oats, corn, rye, barley, beans, peas, potatoes, and tobacco, each in great abundance, and with but little care as to culture. Native fruits grow in great variety, such as the grape, crab-apple, plum, gooseberry, strawberry, and raspberry, each growing in abundance.*

Indiantown contains a population of 200 inhabitants, and is rapidly increasing. The growth and prosperity of the place has been much retarded by the scarcity of lumber, although one of the most extensive bodies of timber in the State adjoins the town on the north, and the water-power afforded by the Iowa, at this point, is unsurpassed in this section. Those who contemplate establishing grist or saw-mills, will do well to investigate the claims and wants of this point. The land is principally owned by actual settlers, who support churches and schools, build bridges and make good roads.

VAN BUREN COUNTY.

The earliest settlements in this county were begun in 1834–5. Keosauqua, the county-seat, was laid out and settled in 1837. The proprietors were Messrs. James

* All that is said of the *productions of the soil* of Tama, will apply to most counties of the State.—Ed.

Hall, John Fairman, John Carns, M. Sigler, and E. Manning.

The population of Keosauqua is about 1500; of the county, by last census, 13,843.

There are two thriving churches, Congregationalist and Methodist, and several other religious societies.

There is one newspaper, the "Democratic Union," published in Keosauqua. No other in the county.

One public school, having from 100 to 120 scholars in attendance. There are also one private school for young ladies, and two high schools, all well patronized and supported; in addition to which, the citizens of Keosauqua contemplate the building of a seminary during the present year.

There are three grist-mills in the town and vicinity, (one water-power and two steam,) and also two saw-mills. The water-power that is now about to be furnished, by the completion of the lock and dam at this place, will not be surpassed in the State.

A woollen manufactory, paper mill, and manufactories of shingles, plows, wagons, and agricultural implements, and also a good merchant flouring-mill, are very much needed. The inducements are readily seen and understood by practical men.

The character of the country may be described as being well divided between prairie and timber. There is a large supply of good timber along the Des Moines River, on both sides. The soil is rich, and produces all the crops congenial to the climate, in the greatest abundance.

The Des Moines improvement, when finished, will afford an uninterrupted navigation to St. Louis and New Orleans; and at present, even without the improvement, we have steamboat navigation from two to four months, during the spring and summer.

Bentonsport contains about 600 inhabitants, supports 2 schools and 2 churches; and has in operation 2 saw-mills, 2 lath mills, 1 flouring mill, 1 paper mill, 1 linseed oil mill, and 1 establishment for manufacturing all kinds of farming implements. Mechanics of all kinds are needed. Farmington, Bonaparte, Vernon, Pleasant Hill, Philadelphia, Portland, New Market and Iowaville, are each prosperous towns, and are becoming points of importance.

Bonaparte also contains a good flouring-mill, two saw-mills, and an extensive brick woollen-factory.

Farmington, below Bonaparte, is also a considerable town, and contains nearly 1000 inhabitants, two or three grist and saw-mills, one foundry, and one engine establishment. There are also several smaller towns in the county, off from the river, some of which are prominent, and rapidly improving.

WAPELLO COUNTY

Was opened to settlement on the 1st of May, 1843, and organized in April, 1844. It is claimed by residents to be one of the best tracts of land in the State. The Des Moines River passes diagonally through the county. The water-power, as furnished by that river and Cedar Creek, is abundant, the banks of the streams also being rich in limestone of the best quality, and excellent sand, which, together with the extensive tracts of timber, render it one of the most desirable counties in the interior of the State. The population of Wapello was 8,466, since which time the county has settled more rapidly than at any previous period. The number of votes polled at the general election in 1854 was 1502.

Ottumwa, the county-seat, is situated at what are called the Appanoose Rapids, on the Des Moines River, distant twenty-five miles from Fairfield, and seven from Agency City, (the old Sac and Fox Agency).

Respecting the Rapids at this place, Mr. Newhall writes: "In August, 1845, a survey of the Appanoose Rapids at this place was made by David Armstrong, Esq., when it was ascertained that there passed at the Rapids, every minute, 42,000 cubic feet of water; a sufficient quantity to fill a lock 42 feet wide, and 150 feet long; being enough to run 28 pair of burrs, 4 feet in diameter, under a head of 6 feet water. There is a fall of 4 feet at these Rapids, in one mile; and a dam, 5 feet high, would give 6 feet 10 inches rise and fall."

Several mills and other manufactories have already been erected at Ottumwa, which place will become one of the most flourishing cities in the interior of the State, when her water-power and other capabilities are fairly developed.

Agency City is situated some seven miles from the centre of the county, and in beauty of locality, and natural scenery, will compare favorably with any point in the interior. The late Indian Agency was here located by

Gen. Street, who considered it a favorable situation in all respects.

Eddyville is situated on the Des Moines River, in the extreme north-west corner of the county, upon the site of an old Indian trading-post. The society in Eddysville is as good as in any place of its size in the State. Churches and schools are well supported, and the edifices and buildings are of a size and character that would do honor to places of greater pretensions.

WAYNE COUNTY

Was organized in 1851,—the first settlements were made in 1848. Corydon, the county-seat, was located in 1852. This section is very sparsely settled, there being but about 500 voters in the county, and less than 100 citizens in Corydon.

Several churches are scattered over the county: Presbyterian, Methodist, Baptist, and Campbellite denominations—two of them Methodist—making a total of five.

The county is well supplied with schools. No newspapers.

With an abundance of excellent water-power, Wayne County invites machinists, capitalists, and manufacturers. No machinery in the county. Timber is not so plenty as in some other counties, but the quality of the land is second to none. Considerable land unentered.

WEBSTER COUNTY.

This is the largest county in the State, containing 921,600 acres of land, comprising what was formely known as Yell, Risley, and the south half of Humboldt. The present population of the county is between three and four thousand. The soil is equal in richness to that of any county in the State—deep and easily worked: in the latter respect, superior to the soil of the southern and middle counties. The surface is gently undulating and in no part broken. The Des Moines River, with its branches, the Boone, Lizara, East and West Forks of the Des Moines, White Fox, and Eagle, with their tributaries, pass through the county in every direction, affording an abundant supply of water for farm use, and water-power unsurpassed in the State. There is a sufficiency of timber on all these streams. Coal is abundant on the Des Moines and Boone rivers, and in the vicinity of Fort Dodge some of the finest beds in the State are found. Also gypsum beds (covering a space of about sixteen square miles), commencing about one mile north of Fort Dodge, and extending about seven miles south on the river) are found. These beds are inexhaustible and of the finest quality. Iron ore, lime-stone of the best quality for lime, and building sandstone, hydraulic limestone, clays, from the coarse material for brick to the fine potter's clay (said by competent judges to be of the best variety), abound. Also varieties of ochre, both yellow and red; springs of as clear, pure water as flow from the rocky beds of Maine are abundant. Improvements are going on rapidly. There are already six water saw-mills, three steam saw-mills, and one grist-mill in the county, and three grist-mills and two saw-mills contracted to be built the coming season. Fort Dodge, Webster City, and Homer, are the principal towns in the county. At Fort Dodge the

Land office is located. There are no church buildings yet erected. In Fort Dodge a literary association is incorporated, with a small library, and a fund of about $300. A lot has been donated by the proprietors of the town, upon which it is the intention of the association to build in a short time.

Webster City (originally called New Castle), is situated 22 miles east of Fort Dodge, on the Dubuque road, has a saw-mill, lath-machine, and other machinery in operation. This being one of the most fertile regions in the State, with an abundance of water-power, and well-timbered, an extensive manufactory of agricultural implements would do well here. The present population of the town is 200.

Homer, the county seat, is situated 19 miles south-east of Ft. Dodge, on the Ft. Des Moines road. Population 300.

Border Plains, 10 miles south of Fort Dodge. Humboldt, 13 miles north of Fort Dodge, in the forks of the East and West branches of the Des Moines River.

Dahkotah is situated 16 miles north of Fort Dodge, and 3 miles north of Humboldt.

WINNEBAGO AND WORTH COUNTIES

Are situated west of Mitchell and east of Kossuth, in the northern tier of counties. Most of the land in these counties is unentered; and no towns have yet been located in either of them.

WINNESHEIK COUNTY

Is bounded on the north by Minnesota, on the east by Alamakee County, on the south by Fayette, and on the west by Chickasaw and Howard Counties. It was occupied by Winnebago Indians until the year 1848, when they were removed by Government. Previous to that time there were no settlers in the county. Fort Atkinson was built about the year 1843, for the protection of the settlements against the incursions of the Indians.

The Old Mission, as it is familiarly called, was formerly a missionary-station, under the patronage of Government. Both the Fort and Mission have been abandoned, and, although in the charge of keepers, are rapidly going to decay. The land about both, comprising 5½ square miles, is still reserved from sale, and is exceedingly fertile.

Among the first settlers may be mentioned Francis Rogers, David Reed, George Ream, William Day, and Wm. Painter. The first settlement was made soon after the removal of the Indians in 1848. The population of the county is estimated at about 5000.

The climate of Winnesheik County resembles that of New York City, although the winters are much shorter, and the autumns very long, mild, and beautiful. The spring generally opens about the 15th of March. The summer is never excessively warm, except where the wind is shut out by the bluffs or timber.

In soil, this county is not excelled. It is a rich black loam, and has a depth of from one to six feet. It has a very slight mixture of sand. Of course, the deepest soil is to be found upon the bottoms. The county is well timbered; about one-fourth of it is heavily timbered, one-third is prairie, and the balance is burr-oak openings, affording plenty of firewood and rails.

The county is well watered by the Upper Iowa, Turkey, and Canoe Rivers, and numerous smaller streams. The Upper Iowa is a beautiful stream, with rock and gravel bed, good banks, swift current, and pure water. The Turkey River, which runs through the south-west part of the county, is also a beautiful stream. The Canoe, which is a branch of the Iowa River, is a fine stream, somewhat smaller than the other two, but all of them afford abundance of mill-power.

Trout Creek is worthy of note. This stream, which is in size about one-third as large as the Upper Iowa, breaks forth in one large spring from the foot of a perpendicular bluff, about two and a half miles from its mouth. It abounds in speckled trout, and is a favorite resort for sportsmen. It rises about two and a half miles south from Decorah, and empties into the Upper Iowa River two miles south-east from that town, at the southernmost bend of the river.

In general, the surface of the country is gently rolling; near the large streams it is bluffy, but the high lands are easily accessible by means of the many ravines running in all directions. The prairies are small, well watered, and agreeably diversified with groves and thickets. Washington, Franklin, and Looking-Glass Prairies are noted for their excellent adaptation to farming purposes.

This county cannot be excelled for stock raising. Sheep

do remarkably well; already there are many flocks of fine blooded ones in the county.

The prevailing rock is lime-stone, which, near the surface, is soft and shelly, but below it is hard and solid. It is always found in layers of a good thickness for building purposes.

Coal is said to have been found in the western part of the county.

There are a number of religious societies formed in the county, among which are Congregationalists, Presbyterians, Methodists, Quakers, and Lutherans.

There are a number of saw-mills, and, although on a small scale, they do a good business. The Decorah saw-mill has one saw which cuts 3000 feet of lumber in twenty-four hours.

There are also a number of grist-mills in the county, doing a thriving business. Decorah grist-mill has two run of stones, which grind 680 bushels of wheat in twenty-four hours.

Dunning's grist-mill, near Decorah, is situated under a large spring, with fifty feet fall of water.

An extensive plow factory has recently been erected in Decorah.

The manufactories most needed at present are: woollen factories, chair factories, sash and door factories, grist-mills, lath-mills, iron foundries, and factories for the manufacture of agricultural implements. The inducements for their erection are the abundance of water-power and materials, and the great demand for their products.

Farmers are much needed—the inducements for them being plenty of vacant land and excellent markets.

Mechanics are very much needed, especially carpenters, masons, millwrights, coopers, saddlers, watchmakers, tinners, cabinet-makers, and painters. The inducements for them are plenty of work and good pay.

Decorah was first settled in the spring of 1849, by Wm. Day, who was followed in June by Wm. Painter. These men for some time were obliged to grind their own flour in a coffee-mill, and bolt it through a sieve. They lived compaparatively alone until the year 1851, when the first saw-mill and store were commenced. The same year a survey was made of a few lots, and the place was called Decorah, after a celebrated Winnebago chief, whose grave is still to be seen at the foot of the beautiful eminence upon which the public buildings of the county are about to be erected. The town was re-surveyed, enlarged, and recorded in 1853, since which it has rapidly improved, and now contains about 800 inhabitants. It commands an extensive trade with Winnesheik, Howard, and Mitchell Counties, and also with a large portion of Minnesota. The business of the place for the past year is estimated at $80,000.

During the last year Decorah has amazingly increased in size, population, and enterprise. The location of the United States Land Office at this place, during the past season, has brought in many energetic business, and wealthy men, and has given the place a start which places it in the foremost rank among the towns of Iowa. The society for the most part is made up of Eastern people; and strangers in search of elevated, polite, and refined society, can find it here. The Decorah common school, numbering 175 scholars, and the Decorah High School, are in a flourishing condition.

Steps are being taken for the immediate erection of the county buildings, and two churches (Methodist and Congregational). Building is constantly going on; midwinter does not stop it, and workmen can hardly spare time to eat their meals or take their nightly rest.

The "Decorah Weekly Chronicle" commenced operations last fall, and is very well sustained.

Daily four-horse coaches connect Decorah with Dubuque, St. Paul, Brownsville, Lansing, McGregor, Clayton, Garnavillo, Guttenburg, Elkader, and West Union, giving the place daily mails in every direction. The Prairie Du Chien and Maukato Air Line Railroad will pass through Decorah, and no doubt is entertained that it will be built at an early day. Decorah has 14 or 15 stores, dealing in the usual variety of merchandise, and yet there is plenty of room for more. Two first class Lawyers are wanted, and none need apply but those who can repeat 40 pages of Kent, one volume of Blackstone, and every word of the "American Lawyer and Form Book." Decorah is supplied with Brokers and Land Agents too numerous to mention.

Of manufactories, Decorah has in operation a steam saw-mill, plow factory, fanning-mill, and machine shop; one saw and two grist mills running by water; one wagon-shop, cabinet-shops, tin-shop — also blacksmiths, shoemakers, saddlers, tailors, milliners, &c.

Freeport,	200 inhabitants,	1 school,	saw and grist mill, &c.
Frankville,	150 "	1 "	steam saw mill.
Bluffton,	75 "	1 "	saw and grist mill.
Cliffton,	50 "	1 "	saw mill.
Burr Oak,	75 "	1 "	
Moneek,	100 "	1 "	saw mill.
Calmar,	50 "		
Hooper,	50 "		steam saw mill.
Enterprise,	30 "		saw mill.
Ossian,	30 "		

(For particulars respecting railroads projected through this country, and the most feasible routes, as well as the locations of streams and minerals, reference is made to "*Parker's Sectional and Geological Map of Iowa.*")

WOODBURY COUNTY

Is situated on the Missouri River, due west from Dubuque County. The first settlement was made in the county in 1853. This county embraces twenty-four whole townships and three fractional townships.

Sergeant's Bluff City is the largest in the county, and the most pleasantly situated town on the Upper Missouri, located on Sec. 25, T. 88, N. Range 48, West. The Bluff from which this town derives its name, is 3 miles above, on the river, where Sergeant Floyd was interred, August 20, 1804, by his companions Lewis and Clarke, while on their expedition to Oregon. Some of the advantages claimed for this point, over others in this section of country, are these :

1. The beauty and healthfulness of the location, and the

good taste and liberality exhibited in the plan of the town. It is divided into wards 1300 feet square, by streets 100 feet wide, crossing each other at right-angles; these wards are divided into blocks by streets 80 feet wide, running parallel with the 100 feet streets. At the crossing of the 100 feet streets there are 4 lots thrown off, forming market squares. In the centre of each ward is a park 280 feet wide by 400 feet long—making, in the area of 600 acres, 8 of those parks, and 15 market squares, besides a suitable levee. The blocks are usually divided into 12 lots, 66 by 132 feet each.

2. It is the natural outlet of the finest portion of the Missouri valley, and the only crossing for the railroads projected west from Dubuque and Clinton, *via* Fort Dodge. Dahkotah, a pleasantly situated town, lies just opposite in Nebraska, and is the "northern gate" of the Territory. This is also the most feasible point for the St. Paul railroad to strike the Missouri, and follow down this valley to St. Joseph's, Mo., and to these considerations, add the fact that this town holds the only Ferry Charter to cross the Missouri River, for five miles south, and twenty miles north, and you will anticipate its future.

3. There is in the vicinity of this town an abundance of building stone, and clay and sand for making brick; large tracts of timber land, and a steam saw-mill and shingle machine, are also in and adjoining the town; which are advantages of importance to those wishing to locate and build.

4. The proprietors propose to donate building lots and furnish a portion of the building materials to actual settlers who will locate and build the present spring. They have also made liberal donations of grounds for the erection of buildings for the North-Western College of Iowa, for the erection of a Congregational and a Methodist church, and for a Female Academy; and one large park, each, to the Odd Fellows, and Masonic Orders—both of these parks to be built upon and ornamented with trees and shrubbery.

Sioux City, is situated 7 miles north of Sergeant's Bluff City, and is the present location of the United States Land Office of the Sioux River District. The greater portion of the land in this district is not yet in market.

Improved lands can be had in Woodbury County at fair prices, and unbroken prairie at government price. The proprietors of these rival towns offer great inducements to mechanics, farmers and capitalists to locate with them. "Professional gentlemen need no invitation, they come West without inducement," says a correspondent in a thrifty western inland town. Mechanics' wages are high and work plenty. (Particulars may be learned of this section of the State, and vacant lands located, by addressing N. H. Parker, at Clinton, Iowa, or Parker and Crocknell, Sergeant's Bluff City, or Parker and Davis, Sioux City.)

WRIGHT COUNTY.

Excellent soil, same character as Webster County. Contains about three or four hundred inhabitants—was organized at the last August election. Otsego is the county-seat. The timber is of good quality, and well distributed along the Boone and Iowa rivers. These two rivers, with their tributaries, afford an abundance of water and water-powers. There are two saw-mills in the county, and improvements are going on rapidly. Stone coal has been found on the Boone River, but to what extent cannot yet be determined. The surface of the county is gently undulating.

CHAPTER XXI.

WESTERN IOWA AND NEBRASKA.

[WE are indebted to the editor of the "*Council Bluffs Eagle*," for most of the matter under this head. The reader will therefore understand which portions of the articles refer to Pottawattamie County, in particular.]

Geography.—That portion of Western Iowa lying west of the Des Moines River, is the most rolling, uneven and picturesque, of the choice lands, in the United States. Although this region is almost entirely composed of hills, swells, ridges, valleys, and bottom lands, thrown together in the most grand and poetic manner, there is scarcely an acre of waste land in the whole region; even the highest points and peaks abound with luxurious grass and vegetation, or timber and copsewood, whilst the slopes, valleys, and bottom lands, together with the upland prairies, are the most rich and fertile ever inhabited.

The soil is a rich, black, light, sandy loam, extremely easy of cultivation, and of a depth of from one to ten feet. Although the soil is naturally extremely light and loose, it resists to a wonderful degree the evil effects of drought upon vegetation. In 1854, when the countries east and south were parched, and crops destroyed for want of rain, ours were remarkably heavy, and seemed uninjured, although we had little or no more rain than our neighbours.

Timber.—There are heavy bodies of hard wood timber on the margin of, and adjacent to, the Des Moines River, and a reasonable quantity interspersed through the counties northwest; yet upon the route directly west to this place, timber is extremely scarce for an hundred miles, being found only in detached groves upon streams: but as one approaches the slope of the Missouri River, the groves and clusters of timber become more frequent, and in this immediate vicinity there is sufficient for all reasonable demands. In several of the counties north, timber is still more abundant, and in Shelby County there is one grove alone that contains nearly thirty square miles of good timber. Through this region generally, there are an abundance of young groves of timber, which, if the fires do not destroy it, will increase quite as fast as the older and more mature portions are used up. The most valuable varieties are oak, (three or four varieties), black walnut, hickory, linn, elm, cottonwood, hackberry, black locust, and coffee bean.

Upon the bottom lands, the cottonwood, black walnut, and elm are found, and in the higher lands, the other varieties.

Minerals.—There is no doubt but that an abundance of coal exists in this region; few beds have, however, yet been opened, but those prove to be of an excellent quality. There are fine quarries of lime-rock, sand and slate-stone.

Climate.—Our climate is similar to that of Northern Ohio, but we have less snow and probably a little more wind. It produces about the same varieties of crops, fruits, and vegetables. The roads are extremely hard and smooth during all the year, except the season of Spring. The evening twilights are long, soft and pleasant, in the Summer season, usually continuing for nearly two hours after sunset. The evenings, even after the hottest days, are usually cool and pleasant. A refreshing breeze is almost constantly blowing from off the prairies.

Wild Fruits and Vegetation.—The wild prairies are covered with a rich, luxurious growth of grass, varying in height from twenty inches to five feet, which makes the finest of grazing, or hay, and which only requires cutting and stacking, not being as liable to injury as the tame grasses. For late feed, the pea-vines and rushes in the low lands, make feed that frequently will keep stock in good order all winter. There are various bulbous roots that grow wild, such as in years past the Indians have gathered for food. Among the best is the wild potatoe, the bean, and artichoke. Hogs eat these voraciously. Among the best of our wild fruits may be reckoned plums, gooseberries, strawberries, raspberries. There are crab apples, and haws, which grow in abundance, and the finest we ever saw. Grapes are of spontaneous growth, and are also fine. The plums are almost as fine as the cultivated varieties—large, delicious and abundant. Strawberries grow around the edges of timber and brushwood, and in the bottoms, along the streams.

Productions. — Corn produces heavily and naturally, yielding from fifty to one hundred bushels to the acre, with little trouble. Winter wheat is not a certain crop, on account of there being so little snow throughout the winter. Spring wheat produces heavily, and of an excellent quality. Oats yield from fifty to seventy-five bushels per acre. Ryê, barley, buckwheat, potatoes, turnips, melons, and other vegetables and grains do well. There are few or no orchards in this region, but there is no doubt that most of the cultivated varieties of fruit will succeed and do well here.

Game, &c.—Elk and deer are abundant in the counties north, and even near here they may be seen every day; there are also abundance of fowls; swan, geese, pelicans, turkeys, ducks, prairie chickens, and quails, abound in their peculiar localities, and fish, of the choicest kinds, fill our lakes and streams. Wild bees are common.

Congress, or Unentered Land.—The most choice lands in this region are entered, but there are within a few miles of the city considerable un-entered lands, which, though without timber, have a good, rich soil. In the country east and north, there remains much to be entered at government price.

Timber lands may also be purchased to suit those who enter prairie lands.

Mills.—We have within this county about twelve saw and grist-mills, but not half enough to supply the demand for lumber and flour. The county above has some four in operation, and the next below, six, and Cass County, one.

In Pottawattamie County we are in extreme need of a good flouring-mill—such as we have in the country will only make from twenty to thirty pounds of flour to the

17*

bushel. How strange! wheat $1 25 per bushel, and flour $5 50 to $6 00 per hundred pounds. Who couldn't make money out of a good mill?

Mechanics.—We are in great want of many and various mechanics, but more especially at this time we have no wagon-makers in Council Bluffs, and it is impossible to get a wagon or carriage mended. If, however, one is so unlucky as to succeed, he will be charged an enormous price, and that by bungling pretenders. Let the mechanics of the east, who are out of employment, (and will soon be out of funds), come here, where they may be serviceable to the community, and get rich. Carpenters, millwrights, brickmakers, masons, engineers, architects, and day labourers, are in special demand.

There are large and small streams at intervals all over the county, the principal of which are the Nishnabotna, Keg Creek, Boyer River, and Musquito and Gopher Creeks. There are a number of lakes in the bottoms, in which, as well as the streams, are stores of excellent fish. Upon these streams are numerous mill sites, only a small proportion of which are occupied. Although there are about one dozen mills already in operation, there is yet a great demand for more, and fortunes might be made by investing money in their erection.

For grazing, stock-growing, or dairy business, there is no region of country better adapted. Stock requires little or sometimes no feed, and upon the prairie grass will fatten in an incredibly short space of time. The poor mechanic and labourer soon become landholders, and the capitalist is not satisfied with less than forty per cent. well secured, which he readily obtains.

How to get here.—Boats run regularly from St. Louis to this place, all through the season of navigation. Freight up usually averages about seventy-five cents per hundred, and passengers (cabin) $15, deck, $5. The railroad from the east is completed to 250 miles from this place. Teams can be purchased in and about Iowa City at fair prices.

Towns.—The largest and most important town west of the Des Moines Valley, is Council Bluffs City, which is located some 3 miles from the Missouri, (directly opposite Omaha City, in Nebraska), is the county-seat of Pottawattamie County, and now contains about 2500 inhabitants. It is a sparsely built incorporated city, contains 2 churches, Methodist and Congregational; 3 schools, 10 stores, 6 doctors, 12 lawyers and mechanics, and artists to match. Lots in the city rate from $100 to $1000, each, and improved farms in the neighborhood from $5 to $10 per acre, including timber. An ever flowing stream, called Indian Creek, runs through the town, and upon the high points of the adjacent bluffs the country for miles around may be seen, including a broad scope of the beautiful and varied lands of Nebraska. A part of the city is laid out with little regularity, it having been settled before the survey of the country; consequently, the lots are of various shapes, and the streets of such angles as will suit the position of the ground. Many excellent buildings already have been, and are now being reared, and good improvements are rapidly progressing. The Land Office for the "Missouri River

District," embracing thirteen counties, is located here. Four distinct railroads have been surveyed to this place from the Mississippi River, from different points, some of which are now actually under course of construction: and it is thought that here will be the great Missouri crossing for the Pacific Railroad.

Improvements, &c.—There are now numerous mills scattered over the whole Missouri slope. In our own county there are some eight or ten saw and grist-mills, but not half enough to supply the wants of the community. Lumber is worth from $25 to $40 per thousand. Many fine farms are opened and cultivated, and the farmers are commencing to improve their farms with a good class of buildings. Farms may be opened at a small expense—a good single ditch can be made for 40 cents per rod, and the prairie broke for about $3 per acre.

A number of towns and cities have sprung up, whose size and population are rapidly increasing; among which, in Frémont County, the county-seat, Sidney, is a handsome and thriving town of 1,000 or 1,200 inhabitants. Coming northward, the next, Tabor, the commencement of a neat county town, is a most thriving and beautiful place, containing a thousand or more inhabitants, with 4 or 5 stores, 2 or 3 public houses, 2 mills, with other necessary business houses and mechanics, is twenty miles south of this city on Keg Creek, and is destined to become an important business town. St. Mary, on the Missouri, and in the same county, a small place, but very prettily situated, has much improved during the past season. This place is opposite Bellevue in Nebraska. Iranistan, in Cass County, forty miles east of this city, on the main stage and railroad route from the east, is a very beautifully located place, on the Nitchnabotna river, has good mills and fine public houses, and must become a nice inland town. Most excellent farms are opened around, and a great spirit of improvement prevails there. As we go north from this city twelve miles, we first come to Americus, a town recently surveyed at Reel's Mills. The proprietor has erected a large and splendid house, which is nearly completed. An excellent and fertile farming country surrounds this place. About twenty-five miles north of this city, on the road to Sergeant's Bluff, in Harrison county, a well-timbered and bountifully watered region, Calhoun, a thriving and fast growing town, is being built, having already some twenty or more houses, most of which have been built this season —two stores are doing a good business there—good farms in the region, and much stock is raised in the vicinity. Magnolia, the county-seat, is also quite a smart place, and promises to become a town of considerable note. Ashton, twenty-five miles above, is a site just surveyed on a beautiful eminence, and surrounded by an excellent agricultural region. Sergeant's Bluff City, still north, and an hundred miles above Council Bluffs, is a young place, situated on the Missouri River. Men of capital and enterprise have gone there to settle, who will make a place out of it, if a good location and energy will do any thing. Sioux City, seven miles further north, on the Missouri River, contains the Land Office for the Sioux River District, is a newly located place and one that bids fair to become a city of great importance. It is on a line directly west of Dubuque, from which place a road is now opened via Fort Dodge. Woodbury County is an excellent agricultural and grazing district, well timbered and abundantly watered, and containing good rock and stone coal. Up the Little Sioux, in the same county, (Woodbury) some seventy-five miles, a flourishing and well located town, called Smithland, is laid out and finely progressing with improvements. A number of towns of less magnitude are laid out and advancing in various parts of Western Iowa, but our limits forbid more special notices at present. This whole region is rapidly becoming populated by the thousands that are coming every month to seize upon the rich and valuable lands, that are waiting to make happy homes for the poor and homeless.

Pottawattomie County is situated on the Missouri River, and is about 42 miles in length on its north line, 36 on its south, and 24 miles wide north and south. It is bounded by Harrison and Shelby Counties on the north, Cass on the east, Mills and a portion of Montgomery on the south, and the Missouri on the west. It contains about 936 square miles, has a population of about 5000, being a trifle less than five and a half to the square mile.

NEBRASKA.

What is said in the foregoing pages of Western Iowa is true, in a great measure, respecting Eastern Nebraska, particularly as to the soil, climate, fruit and vegetation. The western portion of Iowa, and the eastern and southern portions of Nebraska, are not very unlike in these particulars. The interior or western parts are more mountainous and barren, almost entirely destitute of timber, and really of little or no value except for grazing. A number of important towns are springing up on the Missouri River, the most noted, Dahkotah, Omaha City (the capital), Bellevue, Plattsmouth, Mount Vernon, Nebraska City, Florence, Fort Calhoun, De Soto, Tekama, and Fontanelle, occupying a country on the river, north and south, near a hundred miles in extent, and are surrounded with good, fertile, and choice lands. Lime, stone-coal, and other minerals have been found in many places, and this country, though now but little known, offers great inducements to settlers. The capitol being permanently located at Omaha City (opposite Council Bluffs), will make it, eventually, the most important city in the Territory or State. The place is beautifully situated on a high bluff, but the strip of low land intervening between the city and river is almost impassable at times, during high water. Bellevue, nine miles below, is the point at which the Indian Agency for the several tribes in Nebraska Territory is located. The Presbyterian Mission for the Omaha Indians is also located here. Farther than this, the place is at present of not much importance, and not improving as rapidly as some others. The first newspaper ever printed in the Territory, was the "Nebraska Palladium," at Bellevue, in the fall of 1854. Mt. Vernon, at the mouth of the Weeping Water, is one of the most beautiful sites for a town, in the Territory. With an abundance of good building-stone, timber, and stone-coal, surrounded by an excellent farming country, it must eventually become one of the most important towns.

It is the nearest point on the Missouri to the great Salt Springs, in the interior of Nebraska. Nebraska City, eight miles below Mt. Vernon, is a place of some importance, affords a fine view from the river, is surrounded by a fine agricultural country, and from the character of its newspapers, we infer is a place of thrift, energy, and intelligence. This was the site of Old Fort Kearney.

The following is the conclusion of a good-natured letter from one of a company who immigrated to Nebraska, and, finding it wanting, returned to Iowa. Of Nebraska, he says:

" Most of this territory has a very fine soil, and water sufficient in places to make it equal to Iowa, but the almost total absence of timber may keep it back for a great while. On the whole, we are all perfectly convinced that Iowa is the place for us, and hence return well satisfied to stay here. We think that the whole territory put together cannot have one-half the timber that Iowa has.—We also think that there are thousands of acres of unoccupied lands in Iowa, better situated and worth double what many persons are claiming and asking. Nebraska is much better suited for the elk and buffalo, than either for Indian or white man. But the Indians have driven all the former away, and wisely sold it to Uncle Sam, being of no further use to them. We have our fears lest Uncle Sam is bit; but if you believe all the newspaper stories of that region it is certainly a paradise; but Iowa for me forever."

CHAPTER XXII.

PUBLIC LANDS, SYSTEM OF SURVEYS, &C.

The tide of immigration into Iowa last year, and the demand for vacant lands, was unprecedented. We estimate the amount sold at the several Land Offices in 1855, at, say, 10,000,000 acres. Some of this land, when first offered at the newly opened offices, sold as high as $25 per acre. Good land at government price, is comparatively scarce, but there are still large bodies of vacant land in the western and northern portions of the State; and some even within the Coal District of Iowa. This coal field is plainly shown on "*Parker's Sectional and Geological Map of Iowa, for* 1856."

In all the new States and Territories, the lands which are owned by the General Government are surveyed and sold under one general system. The government price of land is $1 25 per acre. The system of surveys is one of great accuracy and beauty. *Meridian* lines are established and surveyed in a line due north from some given point—generally from some important water-course. These are intersected at right angles with a *base* line. On the meridians, the "townships" are numbered north and south from the *base* lines; and, on the *base* lines, "ranges" east or west of the meridian. Township lines are then run at a distance of six miles, parallel to the meridian and base lines. Each township contains an area of 36 square miles; each square mile is termed a section, and contains 640 acres. The sections are numbered from 1 to 36, beginning at the north-east corner of the township, as the following diagram will illustrate:—

6	5	4	3	2	1
7	8	9	10	11	12
18	17	16*	15	14	13
19	20	21	22	23	24
30	29	28	27	26	25
31	32	33	34	35	36

When surveyed, the lands are offered for sale at public auction, but cannot be disposed of at a less price than one dollar and twenty-five cents per acre. That portion not sold at public auction is subject to private entry at any time, for the above price, payable in cash at the time of entry.

Pre-emption rights give the improver or possessor the privilege of purchasing at the minimum price.

I have thus endeavored briefly to elucidate, in the preceding diagram, the system of the surveys of public lands; which, to strangers unacquainted with the sections and subdivisions, appears perplexing and intricate.

* The 16th section in each township is appropriated for schools.

CHAPTER XXIII.

CONSTITUTION OF THE STATE OF IOWA.

(Adopted in Convention, May 18, 1846.)

Preamble and Boundaries.—WE, the People of the Territory of Iowa, grateful to the Supreme Being for the blessings hitherto enjoyed, and feeling our dependence on Him for a continuation of those blessings, do ordain and establish a free and independent government, by the name of the State of Iowa, the boundaries whereof shall be as follows:

Beginning in the middle of the main channel of the Mississippi River, at a point due east of the middle of the mouth of the main channel of the Des Moines River, thence up the middle of the main channel of the said Des Moines River, to a point on said river where the northern boundary line of the State of Missouri, as established by the Constitution of that State, adopted June 12th, 1820, crosses the said middle of the main channel of the said Des Moines River; thence westwardly, along the said northern boundary line of the State of Missouri, as established at the time aforesaid, until an extension of said line intersect the middle of the main channel of the Missouri River; thence up the middle of the main channel of the said Missouri River, to a point opposite the middle of the main channel of the Big Sioux River, according to Nicollett's map; thence up the main channel of the said Big Sioux River, according to said map, until it is intersected by the parallel of forty-three degrees and thirty minutes north latitude; thence east, along said parallel of forty-three degrees and thirty minutes, until said parallel intersect the middle of the main channel of the Mississippi River; thence down the middle of the main channel of said Mississippi River, to the place of beginning.

ARTICLE I.

Bill of Rights.—1. All men are, by nature, free and independent, and have certain inalienable rights, among which are those of enjoying and defending life and liberty, acquiring, possessing, and protecting property, and pursuing and obtaining safety and happiness.

2. All political power is inherent in the people. Government is instituted for the protection, security, and benefit of the people; and they have the right at all times to alter or reform the same, whenever the public good may require it.

3. The General Assembly shall make no law respecting an establishment of religion, or prohibiting the free exercise thereof, nor shall any person be compelled to attend any place of worship, pay tithes, taxes, or other rates, for building or repairing places of worship, or for the maintenance of any minister or ministry.

4. No religious test shall be required as a qualification for any office or public trust, and no person shall be de-

prived of any of his rights, privileges or capacities, or disqualified from the performance of any of his public or private duties, or rendered incompetent to give evidence in any court of law or equity, in consequence of his opinions on the subject of religion.

5. Any citizen of this State, who may hereafter be engaged, either directly or indirectly, in a duel, either as principal or accessory before the fact, shall forever be disqualified from holding any office under the Constitution and laws of this State.

6. All laws of a general nature shall have a uniform operation.

7. Every person may speak, write, and publish his sentiments on all subjects, being responsible for the abuse of that right. No law shall be passed to restrain or abridge the liberty of speech or of the press. In all prosecutions or indictments for libel, the truth may be given in evidence to the jury, and if it appear to the jury that the matter charged as libellous was true, and was published with good motives, and for justifiable ends, the party shall be acquitted.

8. The right of the people to be secure in their persons, houses, papers and effects, against unreasonable seizures and searches, shall not be violated; and no warrant shall issue, but on probable cause, supported by oath or affirmation, particularly describing the place to be searched, and the papers and things to be seized.

9. The right of trial by jury shall remain inviolate; but the General Assembly may authorize trial by a jury of a less number than twelve men in inferior courts.

18*

10. In all criminal prosecutions, the accused shall have a right to a speedy trial, by an impartial jury; to be informed of the accusation against him; to be confronted with the witnesses against him; to have compulsory process for his own witnesses, and to have the assistance of counsel.

11. No person shall be held to answer for a criminal offence, unless on presentment or indictment by a grand jury, except in cases cognizable by justices of the peace, or arising in the army and navy, or in the militia when in actual service, in time of war, or public danger.

12. No person shall, after acquittal, be tried for the same offence. All persons shall, before conviction, be bailable, by sufficient sureties, except for capital offences, where the proof is evident, or the presumption great.

13. The writ of Habeas Corpus shall not be suspended, unless, in case of rebellion or invasion, the public safety requires it.

14. The military shall be subordinate to the civil power. No standing army shall be kept up by the State in time of peace, and in time of war no appropriation for a standing army shall be for a longer time than two years.

15. No soldier shall, in time of peace, be quartered in any house, without the consent of the owner, nor in time of war, except in the manner prescribed by law.

16. Treason against the State shall consist only in levying war against it, adhering to its enemies, or giving them aid and comfort. No person shall be convicted of treason unless on evidence of two witnesses to the same overt act, or confession in open court.

17. Excessive bail shall not be required. Excessive fines shall not be imposed; and cruel and unusual punishments shall not be inflicted.

18. Private property shall not be taken for public use without just compensation.

19. No person shall be imprisoned for debt in any civil action on mesne, or final process, unless in cases of fraud; and no person shall be imprisoned for a militia fine in time of peace.

20. The people have the right freely to assemble together to consult for the common good, to make known their opinions to their representatives, and to petition for redress of grievances.

21. No bill of attainder, ex post facto law, or law impairing the obligation of contracts, shall ever be passed.

22. Foreigners who are, or who may hereafter become residents of this State, shall enjoy the same rights, in respect to the possession, enjoyment, and descent of property, as native born citizens.

23. Neither slavery, nor involuntary servitude, unless for the punishment of crimes, shall ever be tolerated in this State.

24. This enumeration of rights shall not be construed to impair or deny others, retained by the people.

ARTICLE II.

Right of Suffrage.—1. Every white male citizen of the United States, of the age of twenty-one years, who shall have been a resident of the State six months next preceding the election, and the county in which he claims his vote twenty days, shall be entitled to vote at all elections which are now, or hereafter may be authorized by law.

2. Electors shall, in all cases, except treason, felony, or breach of the peace, be privileged from arrest on the days of election, during their attendance at such election, going to, and returning therefrom.

3. No elector shall be obliged to perform militia duty on the day of election, except in time of war, or public danger.

4. No person in the military, naval, or marine service of the United States, shall be considered a resident of this State by being stationed in any garrison, barrack, or military or naval place or station within this State.

5. No idiot or insane person, or persons convicted of any infamous crime, shall be entitled to the privileges of an elector.

6. All elections by the people, shall be by ballot.

ARTICLE III.

Of the Distribution of Power.—1. The powers of the government of Iowa shall be divided into three separate departments; the legislative, the executive, and judicial; and no person charged with the exercise of powers properly belonging to one of these departments, shall exercise any function appertaining to either of the others, except in cases hereinafter expressly directed or permitted.

Legislative Department.—1. The Legislative authority of this State shall be vested in a Senate and House of Representatives, which shall be designated the General Assembly of the State of Iowa, and the style of their laws shall commence in the following manner: "Be it enacted by the General Assembly of the State of Iowa."

2. The sessions of the General Assembly shall be biennial, and shall commence on the first Monday of December next ensuing the election of its members; unless the Governor of the State shall, in the interim, convene the General Assembly by proclamation.

3. The members of the House of Representatives shall be chosen every second year, by the qualified electors of their respective districts, on the first Monday in August, whose term of office shall continue two years from the day of the general election.

4. No person shall be a member of the House of Representatives who shall not have attained the age of twenty-one years; be a free white male citizen of the United States, and have been an inhabitant of this State or Territory one year next preceding his election; and at the time of his election, have an actual residence of thirty days in the county or district he may be chosen to represent.

5. Senators shall be chosen for the term of four years, at the same time and place as Representatives; they shall be twenty-five years of age, and possess the qualifications of Representatives as to residence and citizenship.

6. The number of Senators shall not be less than one-third, nor more than one-half of the Representative body; and at the first session of the General Assembly after this Constitution takes effect, the Senators shall be divided by lot, as equally as may be, into two classes; the seats of the

Senators of the first class shall be vacated at the expiration of the second year, so that one half shall be chosen every two years.

7. When the number of Senators is increased, they shall be annexed by lot to one of the two classes, so as to keep them as nearly equal in number as practicable.

8. Each House shall choose its own officers, and judge of the qualification, election, and return of its own members. A contested election shall be determined in such manner as shall be directed by law.

9. A majority of each House shall constitute a quorum to do business, but a smaller number may adjourn from day to day, and may compel the attendance of absent members, in such manner and under such penalties as each House may provide.

10. Each House shall sit upon its own adjournments, keep a journal of its proceedings, and publish the same; determine its rules of proceedings, punish members for disorderly behaviour, and, with the consent of two-thirds, expel a member, but not a second time for the same offence; and shall have all other powers necessary for a branch of the General Assembly of a free and independent State.

11. Every member of the General Assembly shall have the liberty to dissent from, or protest against, any act or resolution which he may think injurious to the public, or an individual, and have the reasons for his dissent entered on the journals; and the yeas and nays of the members of either House, on any question, shall, at the desire of any two members present, be entered on the journals.

12. Senators and Representatives, in all cases except treason, felony, or breach of the peace, shall be privileged from arrest during the session of the General Assembly, and in going to, and returning from the same.

13. When vacancies occur in either House, the Governor, or the person exercising the functions of Governor, shall issue writs of election to fill such vacancies.

14. The doors of each House shall be open, except on such occasion as, in the opinion of the House, may require secrecy.

15. Neither House shall, without the consent of the other, adjourn for more than three days, nor to any other place than that in which they may be sitting.

16. Bills may originate in either House, except bills for revenue, which shall always originate in the House of Representatives, and may be amended, altered, or rejected by the other; and every bill, having passed both Houses, shall be signed by the Speaker and President of their respective Houses.

17. Every bill which shall have passed the General Assembly shall, before it becomes a law, be presented to the Governor. If he approve, he shall sign it; but if not, he shall return it, with his objections, to the House in which it originated, which shall enter the same upon the journal, and proceed to reconsider it: if, after such reconsideration, it again pass both Houses, by yeas and nays, by a majority of two-thirds of the members of each House present, it shall become a law, notwithstanding the Governor's objections. If any bill shall not be returned within three days after it

shall have been presented to him, Sundays excepted, the same shall be a law in like manner as if he had signed it; unless the General Assembly, by adjournment, prevent such return.

18. An accurate statement of the receipts and expenditures of the public money shall be attached to, and published with the laws, at every regular session of the General Assembly.

19. The House of Representatives shall have the sole power of impeachment, and all impeachments shall be tried by the Senate. When sitting for that purpose, the Senators shall be upon oath or affirmation, and no person shall be convicted without the concurrence of two-thirds of the members present.

20. The Governor, Secretary of State, Auditor, Treasurer, and Judges of the Supreme and District Courts shall be liable to impeachment for any misdemeanor in office; but judgment in such cases shall extend only to removal from office, and disqualification to hold any office of honor, trust, or profit under this State; but the party convicted or acquitted, shall, nevertheless, be liable to indictment, trial, and punishment, according to law. All other civil officers shall be tried for misdemeanors in office in such manner as the General Assembly may provide.

21. No Senator or Representative shall, during the time for which he shall have been elected, be appointed to any civil office of profit under this State, which shall have been created, or the emoluments of which shall have been increased,

during such term, except such offices as may be filled by elections by the people.

22. No person holding any lucrative office under the United States, or this State, or any other power, shall be eligible to the General Assembly: Provided, That offices in the militia, to which there is attached no annual salary, or the office of justice of the peace, or postmasters whose compensation does not exceed one hundred dollars per annum, shall not be deemed lucrative.

23. No person who may hereafter be a collector or holder of public monies, shall have a seat in either house of the General Assembly, or be eligible to any office of trust or profit under this State, until he shall have accounted for, and paid into the treasury, all sums for which he may be liable.

24. No money shall be drawn from the treasury but in consequence of appropriations made by law.

25. Each member of the General Assembly shall receive a compensation, to be fixed by law, for his services, to be paid out of the treasury of the State. Such compensation shall not exceed two dollars per day, for the period of fifty days from the commencement of the session, and shall not exceed the sum of one dollar per day for the remainder of the session. When convened in extra session by the Governor, they shall receive such sum as shall be fixed for the first fifty days of the ordinary session. They shall also receive two dollars for every twenty miles they travel, in going to, and returning from their place of meeting, on the most usual route: Provided, however, That the members

of the first General Assembly under this Constitution shall receive two dollars per day for their services during the entire session.

26. Every law shall embrace but one object, which shall be expressed in the title.

27. No law of the General Assembly, of a public nature, shall take effect until the same shall be published and circulated in the several counties of this State, by authority. If the General Assembly shall deem any law of immediate importance, they may provide that the same shall take effect by publication in newspapers in the State.

28. No divorce shall be granted by the General Assembly.

29. No lottery shall be authorized by this State, nor shall the sale of lottery tickets be allowed.

30. Members of the General Assembly shall, before they enter upon the duties of their respective offices, take and subscribe the following oath or affirmation: "I do solemnly swear, or affirm, (as the case may be,) that I will support the Constitution of the United States, and the Constitution of the State of Iowa, and that I will faithfully discharge the duties of Senator, (or Representative, as the case may be,) according to the best of my ability." And members of the General Assembly are hereby empowered to administer to each other the said oath or affirmation.

31. Within one year after the ratification of this Constitution, and within every subsequent term of two years, for the term of eight years, an enumeration of all the white inhabitants of this State shall be made in such manner as

shall be directed by law. The number of Senators and Representatives shall, at the first regular session of the General Assembly, after such enumeration, be fixed by law, and apportioned among the several counties, according to the number of white inhabitants in each, and shall also, at every subsequent regular session, apportion the House of Representatives, and every other regular session the Senate, for eight years; and the House of Representatives shall never be less than twenty-six, nor greater than thirty-nine, until the number of white inhabitants shall be one hundred and seventy-five thousand; and after that event, at such ratio that the whole number of Representatives shall never be less than thirty-nine, nor exceeding seventy-two.

32. When a Congressional, Senatorial, or Representative district shall be composed of two or more counties, it shall not be entirely separated by any county belonging to another district; and no county shall be divided in forming a Congressional, Senatorial, or Representative district.

33. In all elections by the General Assembly, the members thereof shall vote *viva voce*, and the votes shall be entered on the journal.

34. For the first ten years after the organization of the government, the annual salary of the Governor shall not exceed one thousand dollars; Secretary of State, five hundred dollars; Treasurer, four hundred dollars; Auditor, six hundred dollars; Judges of the Supreme and District Courts, each one thousand dollars.

ARTICLE. IV.

Executive Department.—1. The Supreme Executive power of this State shall be vested in a Chief Magistrate, who shall be styled the Governor of the State of Iowa.

2. The Governor shall be elected by the qualified electors, at the time and place of voting for members of the General Assembly, and shall hold his office four years from the time of his installation, and until his successor shall be qualified.

3. No person shall be eligible to the office of Governor, who has not been a citizen of the United States, and a resident of the State next preceding the election, and attained the age of thirty years at the time of said election.

4. The returns of every election for Governor shall be sealed up and transmitted to the seat of Government, directed to the Speaker of the House of Representatives, who shall, during the first week of the session, open and publish them in presence of both Houses of the General Assembly. The person having the highest number of votes, shall be Governor; but in case any two or more have an equal and the highest number of votes, the General Assembly shall, by joint ballot, choose one of said persons so having an equal and highest number of votes, for Governor.

5. The Governor shall be Commander-in-Chief of the militia, the army and navy of this State.

6. He shall transact all executive business, with the officers of Government, civil and military, and may require information in writing from the officers of the executive

department upon any subject relating to the duties of their respective offices.

7. He shall see that the laws are faithfully executed.

8. When any office shall from any cause become vacant, and no mode is provided by the Constitution and laws for filling such vacancy, the Governor shall have power to fill such vacancy, by granting a commission, which shall expire at the end of the next session of the General Assembly, or at the next election by the people.

9. He may, on extraordinary occasions, convene the General Assembly by proclamation, and shall state to both Houses, when assembled, the purposes for which they shall have been convened.

10. He shall communicate by message to the General Assembly, at every session, the condition of the State, and recommend such matters as he shall deem expedient.

11. In case of disagreement between the two Houses, with respect to the time of adjournment, the Governor shall have power to adjourn the General Assembly to such time as he may think proper, provided it be not beyond the time fixed for the meeting of the next General Assembly.

12. No person shall, while holding any other office under the United States, or this State, execute the office of Governor, except as hereinafter expressly provided.

13. The Governor shall have power to grant reprieves and pardons, and commute punishments after conviction, except in case of impeachment.

14. The Governor shall, at stated times, receive for his services a compensation which shall neither be increased

nor diminished during the time for which he shall have been elected.

15. There shall be a seal of this State, which shall be kept by the Governor, and used by him officially, and shall be called the Great Seal of the State of Iowa.

16. All grants and commissions shall be in the name and by the authority of the people of the State of Iowa, sealed with the great seal of this State, signed by the Governor, and countersigned by the Secretary of State.

17. A Secretary of State, Auditor of Public Accounts, and Treasurer, shall be elected by the qualified electors, who shall continue in office two years. The Secretary of State shall keep a fair register of all the official acts of the Governor, and shall, when required, lay the same, together with all papers, minutes, and vouchers, relative thereto, before either branch of the General Assembly, and shall perform such other duties as shall be assigned him by law.

18. In case of impeachment of the Governor, his removal from office, death, resignation, or absence from the State, the powers and duties of the office shall devolve upon the Secretary of State, until such disability shall cease, or the vacancy be filled.

19. If, during the vacancy of the office of Governor, the Secretary of State shall be impeached, displaced, resign, die, or be absent from the State, the powers and duties of the office of Governor shall devolve upon the President of the Senate; and should a vacancy occur by impeachment, death, resignation, or absence from the State, of the President of the

Senate, the Speaker of the House of Representatives shall act as Governor till the vacancy be filled.

ARTICLE V.

Judicial Department.—1. The Judicial power shall be vested in the Supreme Court, District Courts, and such inferior Courts, as the General Assembly may from time to time establish.

2. The Supreme Court shall consist of a Chief Justice, and two Associates, two of whom shall be a quorum to hold a Court.

3. The Judges of the Supreme Court shall be elected by joint vote of both branches of the General Assembly, and shall hold their Courts at such time and place as the General Assembly may direct, and hold their offices for six years, and until their successors are elected and qualified, and shall be ineligible to any other office during the term for which they may be elected. The Supreme Court shall have appellate jurisdiction only in all cases in chancery, and shall constitute a Court for the correction of errors at law, under such restrictions as the General Assembly may by law prescribe.—The Supreme Court shall have power to issue all writs and process necessary to do justice to parties, and exercise a supervisory control over all inferior judicial tribunals, and the Judges of the Supreme Court shall be conservators of the peace throughout the State.

4. The District Court shall consist of a Judge, who shall be elected by the qualified voters of the district in which he resides, at the township election, and hold his office for the

term of five years, and until his successor is duly elected and qualified, and shall be ineligible to any other office during the term for which he may be elected. The District Court shall be a court of law and equity, and have jurisdiction in all civil and criminal matters arising in their respective districts, in such manner as shall be prescribed by law. The Judges of the District Court shall be conservators of the peace in their respective districts. The first session of the General Assembly shall divide the State into four districts, which may be increased as the exigencies require.

5. The qualified voters of each county shall, at the general election, elect one Prosecuting Attorney, and one Clerk of the District Court, who shall be residents therein, and who shall hold their several offices for the term of two years, and until their successors are elected and qualified.

6. The style of all process shall be "The State of Iowa," and all prosecutions shall be conducted in the name, and by authority of the same.

ARTICLE VI.

Militia.—1. The militia of this State shall be composed of all able-bodied white male citizens, between the ages of eighteen and forty-five years, except such as are, or may hereafter be exempt by the laws of the United States, or of this State, and shall be armed, equipped, and trained as the General Assembly may provide by law.

2. No person or persons, conscientiously scrupulous of bearing arms, shall be compelled to do militia duty, in time

of peace, provided, that such person or persons shall pay an equivalent for such exemption in the same manner as other citizens.

3. All commissioned officers of the militia, (staff officers excepted,) shall be elected by the persons liable to perform military duty, and shall be commissioned by the Governor.

ARTICLE VII.

State Debts.—1. The General Assembly shall not, in any manner create any debt or debts, liability or liabilities, which shall, singly, or in the aggregate, with any previous debts or liabilities, exceed the sum of one hundred thousand dollars, except in case of war, to repel invasion, or suppress insurrection, unless the same shall be authorized by some law for some single object, or work, to be distinctly specified therein, which law shall provide ways and means, exclusive of loans, for the payment of the interest of such debt or liability, as it falls due, and also to pay and discharge the principal of such debt or liability within twenty years from the time of contracting thereof, and shall be irrepealable until the principal and the interest thereon shall be paid and discharged; but no such law shall take effect, until, at a general election, it shall have been submitted to the people, and have received a majority of all the votes cast for and against it, at such election, and all money raised by authority of such law, shall be applied only to the specific object therein stated, or to the payment of the debt thereby created, and such law shall be published in at least one newspaper in each judicial district, if one is published therein, throughout the State, for three months preceding the election, at which it is submitted to the people.

ARTICLE VIII.

Incorporations.—1. No corporate body shall hereafter be created, renewed, or extended, with the privilege of making, issuing, or putting into circulation, any bill, check, ticket, certificate, promissory note, or other paper, or the paper of any bank, to circulate as money. The General Assembly of this State shall prohibit, by law, any person or persons, association, company, or corporation, from exercising the privileges of banking, or creating paper to circulate as money.

2. Corporations shall not be created in this State by special laws, except for political or municipal purposes; but the General Assembly shall provide, by general laws, for the organization of all other corporations, except corporations with banking privileges, the creation of which is prohibited. The stockholders shall be subject to such liabilities and restrictions as shall be provided by law. The State shall not, directly or indirectly, become a stockholder in any corporation.

ARTICLE IX.

Education and School Land.—1. The General Assembly shall provide for the election, by the people, of a Superintendent of Public Instruction, who shall hold his office for three years, and whose duties shall be prescribed by law, and who shall receive such compensation as the General Assembly may direct.

2. The General Assembly shall encourage, by all suitable means, the promotion of intellectual, scientific, moral, and agricultural improvement. The proceeds of all lands that have been, or hereafter may be granted by the United States to this State, for the support of schools, which shall hereafter be sold or disposed of, and the five hundred thousand acres of land granted to the new States, under an act of Congress, distributing the proceeds of the public lands among the several States of the Union, approved A. D. 1841, and all estates of deceased persons, who may have died without leaving a will or heir; and also such per cent. as may be granted by Congress on the sale of lands in this State, shall be, and remain a perpetual fund, the interest of which, together with all the rents of the unsold lands, and such other means as the General Assembly may provide, shall be inviolably appropriated to the support of common schools throughout the State.

3. The General Assembly shall provide for a system of common schools, by which a school shall be kept up, and supported, in each school district, at least three months in every year; and any school district neglecting to keep up, and support such a school, may be deprived of its proportion of the interest of the public fund during such neglect.

4. The money which shall be paid by persons as an equivalent for exemption from military duty, and the clear proceeds of all fines collected in the several counties for any breach of the penal laws, shall be exclusively applied,

in the several counties in which such money is paid, or fine collected, among the several school districts of said counties, in proportion to the number of inhabitants in such districts, to the support of common schools, or the establishment of libraries, as the General Assembly shall, from time to time, provide by law.

5. The General Assembly shall take measures for the protection, improvement, or other disposition of such lands as have been, or may hereafter be reserved or granted by the United States, or any person or persons, to the State for the use of a University; and the funds accruing from the rents or sale of such lands, or from any other source, for the purpose aforesaid, shall be, and remain a permanent fund, the interest of which shall be applied to the support of said University, with such branches as the public convenience may hereafter demand for the promotion of literature, the arts and sciences, as may be authorized by the terms of such grant. And it shall be the duty of the General Assembly, as soon as may be, to provide effectual means for the improvement and permanent security of the funds of said University.

ARTICLE X.

Amendments of the Constitution.—1. If at any time the General Assembly shall think it necessary to revise or amend this Constitution, they shall provide by law for a vote of the people for or against a Convention, at the next ensuing election for members of the General Assembly: in case a majority of the people vote in favor of a Convention, said General Assembly shall provide for an election of Delegates to a Convention, to be held within six months after the vote of the people in favor thereof.

ARTICLE XI.

Miscellaneous. — 1. The jurisdiction of Justices of the Peace shall extend to all civil cases, (except cases in Chancery, and cases where the question of title to any real estate may arise,) where the amount in controversy does not exceed one hundred dollars, and by the consent of parties may be extended to any amount not exceeding five hundred dollars.

2. No new county shall be laid off hereafter, nor old county reduced, to less contents than four hundred and thirty-two square miles.

3. The General Assembly shall not locate any of the public lands, which have been, or may be granted by Congress to this State; and the location of which may be given to the General Assembly, upon lands actually settled, without the consent of the occupant. The extent of the claim of such occupant, so exempted, shall not exceed three hundred and twenty acres.

ARTICLE XII.

Schedule. — 1. That no inconvenience may arise from the change of a Territorial government to a permanent State Government, it is declared that all writs, actions, prosecutions, contracts, claims and rights, shall continue as if no change had taken place in this government; and all process which may, before the organization of the judicial department under this Constitution, be issued under the authority of the Territory of Iowa, shall be as valid as if issued in the name of the State.

2. All the laws now in force in this Territory, which are not repugnant to this Constitution, shall remain in force until they expire by their own limitations, or be altered or repealed by the General Assembly of this State.

3. All fines, penalties, and forfeitures, accruing to the Territory of Iowa, shall accrue to the use of the State.

4. All recognizances heretofore taken, or which may hereafter be taken, before the organization of the judicial department under this Constitution, shall remain valid, and shall pass to, and may be prosecuted in the name of the State. And all bonds executed to the Governor of this Territory, or to any other officer in his official capacity, shall pass over to the Governor of this State, or other proper State authority, and to their successors in office, for the uses therein respectively expressed, and may be sued for, and recovered accordingly. All criminal prosecutions and penal actions, which have arisen, or may arise, before the organization of the judicial department, under this Constitution, and which shall then be pending, may be prosecuted to judgment and execution in the name of the State.

5. All officers, civil and military, now holding their offices and appointments in this Territory, under the authority of the United States, or under the authority of this Territory, shall continue to hold and execute their respective offices and appointments until superseded under this Constitution.

6. The first general election under this Constitution,

shall be held at such time as the Governor of the Territory, by proclamation, may appoint, within three months after its adoption, for the election of a Governor, two Representatives in the Congress of the United States, (unless Congress shall provide for the election of one Representative), members of the General Assembly, and one Auditor, Treasurer, and Secretary of State. Said election shall be conducted in accordance with the existing election laws of this Territory, and said Governor, Representatives in the Congress of the United States, Auditor, Treasurer, and Secretary of State, duly elected at said election, shall continue to discharge the duties of their respective offices for the time prescribed by this Constitution, and until their successors are elected and qualified. The returns of said election shall be made in conformity to the existing laws of this Territory.

7. Until the first enumeration of the inhabitants of this State, as directed by this Constitution, the following shall be the appointment of the General Assembly:

The County of Lee shall be entitled to two Senators, and five Representatives; the County of Van Buren, two Senators, and four Representatives; the Counties of Davis and Appanoose, one Senator, and one Representative, jointly; the Counties of Wapello and Monroe, one Senator, jointly, and one Representative, each; the Counties of Marion, Polk, Dallas, and Jasper, one Senator, and two Representatives, jointly; the County of Des Moines, two Senators, and four Representatives; the County of Jefferson, one Senator, and three Representatives; the County of Henry, one Senator, and three Representatives; the Counties of

Louisa and Washington, one Senator, jointly, and one Representive, each; the Counties of Keokuk and Mahaska, one Senator, jointly, and one Representative, each; the Counties of Muscatine, Johnson, and Iowa, one Senator, and one Representative, jointly; Muscatine, one Representative, and Johnson and Iowa, one Representative, jointly; the Counties of Scott and Clinton, one Senator, jointly, and one Representative, each; the Counties of Cedar, Linn, and Benton, one Senator, jointly; the County of Cedar, one Representative, and the Counties of Linn and Benton, one Representative, jointly; the Counties of Jackson, and Jones, one Senator, and two Representatives; the Counties of Dubuque, Delaware, Clayton, Fayette, Buchanan, and Black Hawk, two Senators, and two Representatives, jointly; and any county attached to any county for judicial purposes, shall, unless otherwise provided for, be considered as forming part of such county for election purposes.

8. The first meeting of the General Assembly, under this Constitution, shall be at such time as the Governor of the Territory may, by proclamation, appoint, within four months after its ratification by the people, at Iowa City, in Johnson County, which place shall be the seat of Government of the State of Iowa, until removed by law.

Done in Convention, at Iowa City, this 18th day of May, in the year of our Lord one thousand eight hundred and forty-six, and of the Independence of the United States the seventieth.

In Testimony Whereof, We have hereunto subscribed our names: ENOS LOWE, *President.*

Attest, WM. THOMPSON, *Sec.*

Thomas Dibble, Erastus Hoskin, David Galland, Sulifand S. Ross, Shepherd Leffler, Curtis Bates, Wm. G. Coop, John Ronalds, Samuel A. Bissell, Socrates H. Tryon, Wareham G. Clark, William Hubbel, John J. Selman, George Berry, John Conrey, Josiah Kent, Joseph H. Hedrick, Sylvester G. Matson, S. B. Shelledy, James Grant, George Hobson, H. P. Haun, Stewart Goodrell, Sanford Harned, David Olmstead, G. W. Bowie, Alvin Saunders, William Steele, T. McCraney, F. K. O'Ferrall, J. Scott Richman.

ORDINANCE.

Be it ordained by the Convention assembled to form a Constitution for the State of Iowa, in behalf of the people of said State, that the following propositions shall be made to the Congress of the United States, which, if assented to by that body, shall be obligatory on this State.

1. Section number sixteen in every surveyed township of public lands, and where such section has been disposed of, other lands, equivalent thereto, and as contiguous as may be, shall be granted to the State for the use of Common Schools.

2. Seventy-two sections of land set apart and reserved for the use and support of a University, by an act of Congress approved on the twentieth of July, one thousand eight hundred and forty, entitled "An act granting two

townships of land for the use of a University in the Territory of Iowa," shall be applied solely for the use and support of such University, in such manner as the General Assembly may direct.

3. That one quarter section of land in each township be granted to the State for the purpose of purchasing a Common School library for the use of such township.

4. That five per cent. of the nett proceeds of the sales of all public lands lying within this State, which shall be sold by Congress after the admission of the State into the Union, shall be granted to the State, for the use of Common Schools.

That, in consideration of the grants specified in the four foregoing propositions, it is declared, that this State will never interfere with the primary disposal of the soil within the same, by the United States, nor with any regulations Congress may find necessary, for securing the title in such soil to the bona fide purchaser thereof; and that no tax shall be imposed on lands, the property of the United States, and that in no case shall non-resident proprietors be taxed higher than resident.

CHAPTER XXIV.

STATE OFFICERS AND CONGRESSMEN, FROM THE ADMISSION INTO THE UNION TO THE PRESENT TIME.

Governor.—*Term, 4 Years.*

	Beginning of Term.
1. Ansel Briggs	November 30, 1846.
2. Stephen Hempstead	December 2, 1850.
3. James W. Grimes	" 3, 1854.

Secretary of State.—*Term, 2 Years.*

1. Elisha Cutler, Jr.	November 30, 1846.
2. Josiah H. Bonney	December 2, 1848.
3. George W. McCleary (3 terms,)	" 2, 1850.

Auditor of State.—*Term, 2 Years.*

1. Joseph T. Fales (2 terms,)	November 30, 1846.
2. William Pattee (2 terms,)	December 2, 1850.
3. A. J. Stevens	" 3, 1854.

Treasurer of State.—*Term, 2 Years.*

1. Morgan Reno (2 terms,)	November 30, 1846.
2. Israel Kister	December 2, 1850.
3. M. L. Morris (2 terms,)	" 2, 1852.

Superintendent of Public Instruction.—*Term, 3 Years.*

	Elected.
1. James Harlan, (election declared illegal,)	April, 1847.
2. Thomas H. Benton, Jr., (2 terms,)	" 1848.
3. James D. Eads	" 1854.

BOARD OF PUBLIC WORKS.—*Term, 2 Years.*

		Elected.
1.	Hugh W. Sample, *President*, ...	August 2, 1847.
1.	Charles Corkery, *Secretary*, ...	" "
1.	Paul Bratton, *Treasurer*, ...	" "
2.	William Patterson, *President*, ...	" 6, 1849.
2.	Jesse Williams, *Secretary*, ...	" "
3.	George Gillaspy, *Treasurer*, ...	" "

The second Board was legislated out of office on the 1st of February, 1851.

COMMISSIONER AND REGISTER OF THE DES MOINES RIVER IMPROVEMENT.—*Term, 2 Years.*

1. V. P. Antwerp, *Commissioner*, ... appointed from Feb. 1, 1853.
2. Josiah H. Bonney, " .... elected, April 4, 1853.
1. George Gillaspy, *Register*, ... appointed, February 1, 1851.
2. Paul Jeffers, " .... " " 1852.
3. George Gillaspy, " .... elected, April 4, 1853.

ATTORNEY-GENERAL.—*Term, 2 Years.*

1. D. C. Cloud .... August 1, 1853.
2. " .... August 7, 1854.

THE EXECUTIVE, IN 1855.

JAMES W. GRIMES, of Burlington, *Governor*.
George W. McCleary, Iowa City, *Secretary of State*.
John Pattee, Fort Des Moines, *Auditor*.
M. L. Morris, Iowa City, *Treasurer*.
James D. Eads, Iowa City, *Superintendent of Public Instruction*.
D. C. Cloud, Muscatine, *Attorney-General*.
Wm. McKay, *Commissioner of the Des Moines River Improvement*.
John C. Lockwood, *Register of the Des Moines River Improvement*.
Anson Hart, *Register of the Land Office*.

THE LEGISLATURE.

Maturin L. Fisher, *President of the Senate*.
Reuben Noble, *Speaker of the House of Representatives*.

CONGRESSIONAL DELEGATION.

George W. Jones, of Dubuque, *Senator*, ... Term expires, 1859.
James Harlan, of Mt. Pleasant, " ...... " " 1861.
Augustus Hall, of Keosauqua, *Representative.*
James Thorington, of Davenport, "

THE JUDICIARY.

Supreme Court.

George G. Wright, Keosauqua, *Chief Justice.*
W. G. Woodward, Muscatine, *Associate Justice.*
N. W. Isbell, Marion, " "
William Vandever, Iowa City, *Clerk.*

District Court for Iowa.

J. M. Love, of Dubuque, *Judge.*
J. C. Knapp, of Keosauqua, *District Attorney.*
Laurel Summers, of Le Claire, *Marshal.*
Warner Lewis, of Dubuque, *Surveyor-General.*

Note.—The election for Governor, State Officers, and Board of Public Works is held on the first Monday in August. The term of service of the Governor and State Officers commences on the first Monday in December following the election.

Times of Holding Elections.

1. *General Election*—Is held 1st Monday in August, every two years. Time of holding next General Election will be August, 1856. Officers elected: A Governor, once in four years; a State Senator, once in four years; a Secretary, Treasurer, and Auditor of State, Prosecuting Attorney, Clerk of the District Court, Representatives to the General Assembly, and Representatives to Congress, every two years.

2. *August Election*—Is held 1st Monday in August, every two years, alternate with the years of the General Election. Officers elected: County Judge, once in two years; Sheriff, Coroner, Recorder, and Surveyor, every two years.

3. *April Election*—Is held annually, 1st Monday in April. Officers elected: Judge of District Court, once in five years; Superintendent of Public Instruction, once in three years; School Fund Commissioner, once in two years; three Township Trustees, a Clerk, two Constables, and an Assessor, every year; two Justices of the Peace (or as many as the Trustees of each township may direct,) every two years (one being elected each year).

4. *Presidential Election*—Is holden 1st Tuesday after the 1st Monday in November, 1856, and every four years thereafter, for the election of Electors of President and Vice-President of the United States, the number of whom is equal to the number of Senators and Representatives in Congress to which this State may be entitled.

5. *City Elections*—Held at such times as fixed by the charter, or as regulated by ordinance; electing Mayor, Marshal, Clerk, Treasurer, and Aldermen.

CHAPTER XXV.

JUDICIAL DISTRICTS.—TIMES OF HOLDING COURTS.

First District.—Composed of the counties of Lee, Des Moines, Louisa, and Henry. Term of court held:

In Lee County, at Keokuk, on the second Monday of February, and the first Monday of September.

At Fort Madison, on the first Tuesday after the first Monday in April, and the fourth Monday in October.

In Des Moines, on the fourth Monday in April, and the second Monday in November.

In Louisa, on the second Monday in March, and the first Monday in October.

In Henry, on the third Monday in March, and the second Monday in October.

Second District.—Consisting of the counties of Dubuque, Delaware, Clayton, Alamakee, Winneshiek, Fayette, Buchanan, Black Hawk, Bremer, Chickasaw, and Howard. Terms of Court are held:

In the County of Dubuque, on the first Monday in October, and the fourth Monday in March.

In the County of Clayton, on the fourth Mondays in May and October.

In the County of Alamakee, on the first Mondays in June and November.

In the County of Fayette, on the second Mondays in June and November.

In the County of Delaware, on the third Mondays in June and November, and in all other counties at such times and places as the judge may direct.

Third District.—Terms of Court, as follows, in the Third District:

In the County of Mahaska, on the first Monday in February, and first Monday in September.

In the County of Wapello, on the fourth Monday in February, and fourth Monday in September.

In the County of Davis, on the second Monday after the fourth Monday in February, and on the second Monday in October.

In the County of Van Buren, on the fourth Monday after the fourth Monday of February, and on the fourth Monday of October.

In the County of Jefferson, on the second Monday in April and November.

In the County of Keokuk, on the fourth Monday in April, and on the third Monday in September.

Fourth District.—Times of holding Court as follows:

In the County of Johnson, on the first Monday of February and June, and second Monday in October.

In the County of Linn, on the first Monday in April and September.

In the County of Benton, on the third Monday in April and September.

In the County of Washington, on the fourth Mondays in April and September.

In the County of Iowa, on the first Monday in May, and the fourth Monday in October.

In the County of Poweshiek, on the third Monday in May.

In the County of Tama, on the first Tuesday after the third Monday in May.

Fifth District.—In the County of Marion, on the second Monday in February, and fourth Monday in August.

In the County of Polk, on the third Monday in March, and the second Monday in August.

In the County of Jasper, on the second Monday in April and September.

In the County of Marshall, on the third Monday in April and September.

In the County of Hardin, on the fourth Monday in April.

In the County of Story, on the first Monday in May.

In the County of Boone, on the second Monday in May and the fourth Monday in September.

In the County of Webster, on the first Monday in October.

In the County of Greene, on the third Monday in May.

In the County of Dallas, on the fourth Monday in May, and the second Monday in October.

Sixth and Seventh Districts.—In the County of Fremont, on the first Monday in March and September.

In the County of Page, on the fourth Monday in March and September.

In the County of Taylor, on the Thursday after the fourth Monday of March and September.

In the County of Adams, on the first Monday in April and October.

In the County of Guthrie, on the second Monday in April and October.

In the County of Cass, on the Thursday after the second Monday in April and October.

In the County of Mills, on the second Monday in March and September.

In the County of Pottawattamie, on the first Monday in April and October.

In the County of Harrison, on the first Monday in May and November.

In the County of Shelby, on the Thursday after the first Monday in May and November.

In the County of Woodbury, on the first Monday in September.

In all other counties at such time and place as the Judge may appoint.

Eighth District.—Composed of the counties of Muscatine, Scott, Cedar, Jones, Clinton, and Jackson.

In the County of Jackson, on the fourth Monday in April, and second Monday in September.

In the County of Clinton, on the first Monday after the fourth Monday in April, and third Monday in September.

In the County of Cedar, on the second Monday after the fourth Monday in April, and fourth Monday in September.

In the County of Scott, on the third Monday after the fourth Monday in April, and first Monday after the fourth Monday in September.

In the County of Muscatine, on the fourth Monday after the first Monday in April, and second Monday after the fourth Monday in September.

Ninth District.—Composed of the counties of Monroe, Appanoose, Wayne, Decatur, Lucas, Clarke, Warren, and Madison.

In the County of Monroe, on the third Monday in April, and first Monday in September.

In the County of Appanoose, on the second Monday after the third Monday in April, and third Monday in September.

In the County of Wayne, on the fourth Monday after the third Monday in April, and the second Monday after the third Monday in September.

In the County of Decatur, on the fifth Monday after the third Monday in April, and third Monday after the third Monday in September.

In the County of Clark, on the sixth Monday after the third Monday in April, and fourth Monday after the third Monday in September.

In the County of Madison, on the seventh Monday after the third Monday in April, and fifth Monday after the third Monday in September.

In the County of Warren, on the eighth Monday after the third Monday in April, and the sixth Monday after the third Monday in September.

In the County of Lucas, on the ninth Monday after the third Monday in April, and the seventh Monday after the third Monday in September.

Tenth District.—Composed of the counties of Clayton, Alamakee, Winnesheik, Fayette, Chickasaw, Floyd, Mitchell, Howard, Worth, and Cerro Gordo.

In the County of Clayton, on the third Monday in May and October.

In the County of Fayette, on the first Monday after the third Monday in May and October.

In the County of Chickasaw, on the second Monday after the third Monday in May and October.

In the County of Floyd, on the third Monday after the third Monday in May and October.

In the County of Winnesheik, on the fourth Monday after the third Monday in May and October.

In the County of Alamakee, on the fifth Monday after the third Monday in May and October.

CHAPTER XXVI.

EDUCATION.

School System.—A very liberal provision is made for the permanent support of common and academic institutions in this State. By an act of Congress, 500,000 acres of land have been set apart for the promotion of the cause of education. Some of these lands have been sold, and the proceeds safely invested for the use of schools. Much, however, remains in the market, and will be disposed of as the wants and interests of these nurseries of knowledge demand.

There is about $1,000,000 in the hands of the School Fund Commissioners, within the State, which is loaned at ten per cent., yielding an income of nearly $100,000. This amount, distributed among the schools, places them upon a footing not surpassed by any new State in the north-west.

State University of Iowa.

This institution opened on the third Wednesday of September. It has been permanently located at Iowa City, the site of the Capitol, and is to have the use of the public buildings, together with ten acres of land, on which they are situated. Two townships of land, granted by act of Congress, July 20th, 1840, for the support of a university, have been donated by the State to this institution, and constitute a permanent fund, for its support.

The following advantages are possessed by this institution:

1st. It is the People's Institution, and every citizen of the State is interested in it.

2d. It is entirely free from sectarian influence and bias.

3d. It has an endowment of between $175,000 and $200,000, which places it upon a basis second to none in the Union, and enables the trustees to sustain a competent number of efficient and educated men in the faculty.

4th. Its library and apparatus, when complete, (probably during this year), will be superior to any in the West.

5th. It is favourably located, in respect to health, good society, and beautiful and romantic scenery.

Faculty.

AMOS DEAN, LL. D., President, and Professor of History. ALEX. JOHNSTON, A. M., Professor of Mathematics. HENRY S. WELTON, A. M., Professor of Ancient Languages. JAMES HALL, Professor of Natural History. JOSIAH D. WHITNEY, Professor of Chemistry. E. M. GUFFIN, A. M., Preparatory Department. JOHN VANVALKENBERG, Normal School.

There is a Normal School connected with the University, to which fifty students are entitled to go free of charge, by receiving an appointment from the Governor, Superintendent of Public Instruction, or from either of the District Judges. The State University is amply endowed, so that all may be admitted free, but probably not the first year.

Branch at Fairfield.—One branch of the State University is established at Fairfield, Jefferson County, and is put upon the same footing with respect to funds and other details, as the present Seminary.

Branch at Dubuque.—Another branch of the State University is to be established at Dubuque. The trustees have been appointed, the site selected, and most of the measures necessary to the enterprise taken.

Normal Schools.—The State is divided into three districts, in each of which there was to be established a Normal School, for the education of teachers for our common schools. The law establishing these schools, located them at Oskaloosa, Mount Pleasant, and Andrew.

District Schools.—Of these, Jas. D. Eads, Esq., late State Superintendent, says: "In many of the older counties that I have travelled through, the citizens have gone to work with a liberal and praiseworthy spirit, in erecting large and commodious buildings for educational purposes. The city of Keokuk takes the lead in having the finest building in the State, in the erection of which the citizens have expended nearly ten thousand dollars; and with a liberal spirit, they pay the Superintendent of the school eight hundred dollars per annum.

"Fort Madison, Burlington, Muscatine, Davenport, Lyons, Anamosa, Colesburgh, Marion, Rochester, Tipton, Denmark, Primrose, West Point, Centreville, Oskaloosa, Cedar Falls, and many other towns, have erected buildings which will stand as lasting monuments of the liberality of those engaged in so glorious an enterprise, and an honour to our young State.

"Iowa, young as she is, already commands a prominent position, not only in reference to the magnitude of her School Fund, but in the progress she has made in the organization of her districts, and the general establishment of free schools.

"According to the returns of the County Commissioners, there are twenty-three hundred and fifty-five organized school districts in Iowa, and over one hundred and eleven thousand children between the ages of five and twenty-one years. When we consider, in connection with these facts, that our population is increasing with a rapidity almost unparalleled in the history of any country, and that in a very few years we shall equal in numbers the most populous of the Eastern States, it becomes apparent that we cannot be too active and vigilant in all that pertains to the education of the youth of our State, who are so soon to control the destiny of a great Commonwealth.

"While we congratulate ourselves upon the possession of so magnificent a school fund, as has been secured to us by the action of the General Government, and our State Legislature, we must not forget that much remains to be done on the part of the people themselves, before we shall fully enjoy the advantages of a universal system of free schools, of a character commensurate with the object of their organization, viz.: to give to every son and daughter of Iowa a thorough knowledge of all the essential elements of a good practical education.

"I have had the pleasure, during the past season, of visiting a large number of union or graded schools, in the larger towns of the State, and have been very highly gratified in witnessing the many advantages they possess, when properly conducted, over those schools which maintain separate organizations.

"As appears from the returns of the County Commissioners, the average sum paid to the district school teacher is less than twenty dollars to the male, and less than ten dollars per month to female teachers."

In all the thickly settled counties, common schools are convenient, and should the tide of immigration continue to flow as it has done, in five years not one county in ten will be destitute of the facilities for a sound education. The number and condition of public schools are given more particularly in the sketches of the counties, in another portion of this work.

Deaf and Dumb, and Blind Asylums.—Institutions for the instruction of these unfortunate citizens, were organized in 1853, and have since been in successful operation in Iowa City. Appropriations of $5000 for the support of the Deaf and Dumb, and of $6000 for the support of the Blind Institutions, have been made, and the trustees have rented suitable buildings.

The number of deaf and dumb pupils admitted is 32—of blind, 23.

These institutions bid fair to do great service, even the present year, in extending to this unfortunate class, the light and knowledge which, but for education, they must be deprived of.

Academies and Colleges.—This State is well supplied with acadamies and colleges, some of which will compare favorably with those in the Atlantic States, while *all* reflect credit upon the patriotism and enterprise of the Hawkeye State. We give herein a sketch of the condition of those of the principal schools of this class, concerning which we have been able to gain satisfactory data :—

The Burlington University.—This is a literary institution of the Baptist denomination, located at Burlington, in April, 1852. The college edifice was erected in 1853–4, and dedicated on the 4th of July, 1854. This building is 44 by 65 feet, three stories high, and its style of architecture and economic arrangement reflect great credit upon its founders and architects. The first annual catalogue of the institution was issued on the first of January, 1855, which reports 167 pupils, and a faculty of eight different teachers, with Geo. W. Gunnison, A. M., as principal. The school is now in a flourishing condition. The institution possesses available property to the amount of $20,000, and is nearly free from debt, besides $5000 secured and drawing interest, as the commencement towards a fund for enlarging their buildings. The plan of the institution provides for preparatory and collegiate departments, with courses of study for gentlemen and ladies. The gentlemen's course embraces 7 years—3 preparatory, and 4 collegiate; the ladies' 5 years—1 primary, and 4 advanced. Those desiring further information of the institution, may address the Principal, at Burlington, or Rev. Jas. A. Nash, President of the Board of Trustees, at Ft. Des Moines.

Alexander College

Has been recently established, at Dubuque, under the patronage of the Synod of Iowa, but is not intended to be sectarian in its influence. A new college building was erected last year, 60 feet wide by 100 feet long, and four stories high, including basement; computed cost, upwards of $15,000. The ground occupied by this College embraces three acres, on the bluff one mile west from Main Street—a high, healthy, and in every respect desirable location. Situated in the midst of a vast region of country teeming with the elements of material wealth, and rapidly filling up with an intelligent and enterprising people, this College cannot but succeed.

The Central College of Iowa

Is pleasantly situated in a healthy location, at Fort Des Moines, and bids fair to become an institution of the highest order. It is under the fostering care of the Lutheran Church, but is not sectarian in its character. The aim of the faculty will be to exert a healthy moral influence upon the student, and to secure to him a complete and finished education. The main college building will be erected this season, at a cost of $20,000. For further particulars, address R. Weiser, President, Fort Des Moines.

The Central University of Iowa.

An institution under the direction and patronage of the Baptist Church of Iowa, is located at Pella, Marion County. A large and substantial brick edifice is in course of erection, and will be completed in June, we understand. The number of students in attendance in 1855, was 122. H. P. Scholte, President; M. A. Clark, Secretary; E. H. Scarff, Principal.

The Dubuque Female Institute

Is delightfully situated upon a natural terrace—a high bluff rising in the background—in the foreground lies the beautiful and rapidly growing city of Dubuque, whose wharves and levee are washed by the noble Mississippi, bearing on its bosom the rich products of this fruitful land. The large and substantial brick edifice of this Institute, cost $16,000. The Institution was established three years since, under the patronage of Miss Catharine Beecher, and offers every advantage to pupils which can be enjoyed in any similar one in the West.

Iowa College.

This College, founded in 1848, under the auspices of the New School Presbyterians and Congregationalists, is located in the north part of the City of Davenport.

The grounds upon which it is built consist of ten acres of land, lying upon the bluff, beautifully adorned with a young and thriving grove, and commanding a most delightful prospect of the prairies on the north, and of the Mississippi River, with the adjacent cities on the south.

The new building is now occupied for college purposes. It is constructed of limestone of the most durable quality. It has three stories, containing a large assembly-room, a laboratory, rooms for library, cabinet, apparatus, literary societies, and recitation rooms. The third story is divided into rooms for students. There is also a spacious basement for fuel and furnaces. The expense of this substantial, yet elegant, structure is about $20,000.

The College boarding-house stands upon the premises, at which board is furnished to students at $1.50 per week, and room rent at $2.00 per term.

The Institution, as now arranged, has three departments, English, preparatory, and collegiate, in each of which the course of instruction is ample and thorough. The Faculty consists of—

Rev. E. Ripley, Professor of Ancient Languages.

Rev. H. L. Bullen, Professor of Mathematics and Natural Philosophy.

D. S. Sheldon, Professor of Chemistry and Natural Science.

Rev. D. Lane, Professor of Mental and Moral Philosophy.

The number of students last year was one hundred.

The library of the college is open to all departments.

Apparatus is provided for the illustration of Natural Philosophy, Physiology, Chemistry, Surveying, and Astronomy. Collections in Botany, Zoology, and Mineralogy have been commenced.

The Iowa Conference Seminary,

Located at Mount Vernon, Linn County, has a brick edifice 40 by 72 feet, 3 stories high. This Institution is in a very prosperous condition, under the superintendence of Rev. S. M. Fellows, A. M., assisted by three regular teachers, besides a female teacher of music, painting and embroidery. This seminary is well sustained, and the trustees contemplate erecting a new college edifice, 50 by 120 feet, four stories high. Mount Vernon is very pleasantly located, in a rich agricultural district, well settled, by intelligent and industrious people.

The Iowa Wesleyan University,

Under the control of the M. E. Church, is located at Mount Pleasant, Henry County, one of the most pleasant and healthy locations in the State, and in the midst of an intelligent and refined community. This is a first-class collegiate institute, with an able faculty, and had an attendance last year of 254. The University building is large and commodious, 3 stories high, situated upon grounds laid out in a very handsome style, and ornamented with beautiful trees and fine shrubbery. (See Iowa Medical College.)

The Mount Pleasant High School and Female Academy, with an average attendance of 100 pupils, is also in a prosperous condition, and worthy the liberal patronage it receives.

Iowa Medical College, Keokuk.

This institution has been adopted as the Medical Department of the Iowa Wesleyan University. The first term under the new arrangement, opened on the first Monday of November last, with flattering prospects. Particulars of terms, &c., together with all desired information, may be obtained by addressing Hon. Thos. W. Claggett, President.

Female College, under the auspices of the I. O. O. F. of Iowa.

The State Lunatic Asylum has been located at Mount Pleasant, and the requisite buildings will soon be erected there.

The Christian Church of Iowa, have also decided upon Mount Pleasant, as the most eligible location for their College, and we presume the buildings will be erected this year.

Iowa Female Collegiate Institute, at Iowa City, under the auspices of the I. O. of O. F.

"Articles of incorporation were adopted and recorded on the 29th of July, 1853, which place the institution under the particular auspices of the Independent Order of Odd Fellows of Iowa, and secures in the instruction and government of the school the same broad and liberal basis, and the same freedom from every species of sectarianism, which distinguishes that Order.

"It also offers to all Lodges and Encampments, contributing one hundred dollars to the funds of the institution, a perpetual scholarship; and to each individual contributor of the same amount, a scholarship for twenty years, or during his natural life. By this arrangement we hope to be able, at some future day, to offer *free instruction* to all *poor* orphan daughters of the Order in the State. This, indeed, is a primary object had in view by the Board in the establishment of their institution, and will not be lost sight of in their future plans and labor for the permanent organization of their school.

"During the past year the attention of the Board has been directed chiefly towards the collection of funds, and to the preparations for the erection of a suitable College edifice for the use of the institution.

"In this effort, very gratifying success has rewarded their labor. Notwithstanding the protracted illness of their agent has deprived the Board of his services for nearly one-half of the past year, yet they are happy to report the collection of about $8000 in cash, notes, valid subscriptions, and other property, as the result of their efforts.

"The City Council at Iowa City, at their regular meeting in September, 1853, donated to the Board an eligible site for their College edifice; and the Grand Lodge of the I. O. of O. F. of the State of Iowa laid the corner-stone of the College, October 27th, 1853, with the usual ceremonies of the Order."

The edifice will be completed and ready for occupation at an early day.

For further particulars address F. H. Lee, Secretary, Iowa City.

See particulars of "Iowa Conference Seminary," of Mt. Vernon, and of the "Iowa Wesleyan University," "Mt. Pleasant High School and Female Academy," in the sketches of Linn and Henry counties.

"Ladies, College."

The above is the name of an educational institution, which was established in 1855, in the city of Davenport, under the direction of T. H. Codding, Esq., who is also

Ladies' College, Davenport.

its proprietor. The building, when completed, at a cost of $20,000, will present a front of 120 feet, and four stories in height, with a depth of 80 feet. The main building was opened for the reception of scholars on the first of May. Upon the selection of the site for the "Ladies' College," too much praise can scarcely be bestowed. Standing upon a lofty bluff, it commands a sweep of landscape scarce excelled throughout the region of the Upper Mississippi, while the broad summit of the hill, whose centre it decks, affords ample room for extensive promenades, and the gentle slopes which decline towards the lowlands, render it easy of access to pedestrians and carriages.

The "Ladies' College" aims to prepare young ladies for the active practical duties of life, by a judicious combination of mental, moral, and physical training. Its proprietor says:

"The course of instruction will be thorough, complete, discriminating and select, avoiding everything of a useless character, and substituting those branches whose tendency is to give vigor and elasticity to the youthful mind.

"The manner of teaching will be the most *approved* and *improved* known in our country or in Europe, giving the pupil the full understanding of her subject, while it is presented by the teacher in a new and fascinating style."

To insure to pupils a thorough English and classical education, and familiarity with the languages, a large corps of experienced and accomplished teachers have been engaged as assistants to Mr. T. H. Codding and Mrs. O. Codding, the Principals and Superintendents of the Institute. The fourth quarter commenced Feb. 20th, 1856.

CHAPTER XXVII.

RELIGIOUS WORSHIP.

Congregational Churches.—The State of Iowa is divided into five associations. The latest reports are from the proceedings of the annual Association, in June, 1854, as follows:—

	No. of Members.
Council Bluffs Association,	94
Davenport "	615
Denmark "	759
Des Moines River "	364
Dubuque "	657
	2489
Members new churches not included..........	188
	2677

No. of Ministers in the State,			73
" Churches	"	"	89
Meeting Houses	"	"	44
" building	"	"	5

Congregational churches are thus located: *Council Bluffs Association.*—Civil Bend, Council Bluffs, Tabor, (Florence, N. T.). *Davenport Association.*—Anamosa, Copper Creek, Davenport, Deep Creek, De Witt, Le Claire, Lyons, Marion, Muscatine, Sabula, Sterling, Sugar Creek, Summit, Tipton, Toledo. *Denmark Association.*—Brighton, Burlington, Clay, Columbus, Crawfordsville, Danville, Denmark, Flint, Hillsboro', Long Creek, Mount Pleasant North Marion, Old Man's Creek, Salem, Trenton, Wapello, Warren, Wayne. *Des Moines River Association.*—Bentonsport, Chariton, Eddyville, Elk Creek, Fairfield, Farmington, Keosauqua, Knoxsville, Marysville, Oskaloosa, Ottumwa, Pleasantville, Red Rock. *Dubuque Association.*—Bellevue, Bowen's Prairie, Cascade, Centre, Colesburg, Cottonville, Decorah, Dubuque, Durango, Farmersburgh, French Settlement, Garnaville, Lansing, Manona, Maquoketa, Quasqueton, Sherold's Mound, Teroli, West Union, Yankee Settlement.

Statistical Table of Baptists in Iowa.

Associations.	Churches.	Pastors.	Baptised during year.	No. of Members.	Date of Report.
Des Moines	21	11	247	1159	Aug. 25, 1854.
Davenport	24	17	73	1078	Sept. 15, 1854.
Oskaloosa	16	5	32	502	Aug. 30, 1854.
Central Iowa	14	6	98	384	Sept. 29, 1854.
Fox River	17	7	69	628	Sept. 8, 1854.
Eden	10	3		300	
6 Associations	102	49	519	4051	
Not included in above	3	11		49	A low estimate.
	105	60	519	4100	

Statistical History of the Iowa Baptist Convention.

Anniver'y.	Where Held.	Moderator.	Clerk.	In. Preacher.
1st—1842.	Iowa City,	Rev. B. Carpenter,	Rev. W. B. Morey,	Rev. H. Johnson.
2d—1843.	Davenport,	Rev. H. Johnson,	J. T. Fales,	" A. Sherwood.
3d—1844.	Mt. Pleasant,	Rev. E. Fisher,	C. G. Blood,	" C. E Brown.
4th—1845.	Bloomington,	Rev. H. Burnett,	Rev. C. E. Brown,	" W. B. Morey.
5th—1846.	Iowa City,	Rev. B. F. Brabrook,	J. T. Fales,	" J. N. Seely.
6th—1847.	Farmington,	J. T. Fales, Esq.,	Rev. W. B. Morey,	" H. Burnett.
7th—1848.	Davenport,	Rev. D. P. Smith,	Rev. T. H. Archibald,	" D. P. Smith.
8th—1849.	Iowa City,	Rev. B. F. Brabrook,	Rev. T H. Archibald,	" C. E. Brown.
9th—1850.	Mt. Pleasant,	Rev. D. P. Smith,	Rev. S. B. Johnson,	" T. H. Archibald.
10th } 1 ses	Muscatine,	J. T. Fales, Esq.,	Rev. S. B. Johnson,	" G. J. Johnson.
1851 } 2 ses	Burlington,	J. T. Fales, Esq.,	Rev. S. B. Johnson,	" W. A. Wells.
11th—1852.	Marion,	Rev. E. Gunn,	Rev. I. C. Curtis,	" J. A. Nash.
12th—1853.	Keokuk,	Rev. E. M. Miles,	Rev. Wm. Turton,	" G. J. Johnson.
13th—1854.	Davenport,	Rev. H. Burnett,	Rev. H. R. Wilbur,	" W. Elliott.

SYNOD OF IOWA. (N. S.)

The Synod of Iowa consists of four Presbyteries, as follows:

1. *The Presbytery of Des Moines*, with the churches of Fort Des Moines, Winterset, Mount Gideon, Bloomfield, Centreville, Union, Troy, Shunem, and Three Rivers.

2. *The Presbytery of Keokuk*, with the churches of Keokuk, Oskaloosa, Croton, Pleasant Grove, Montrose, Pisgah, Fort Madison, Yellow Spring and Toolesborough.

3. *The Presbytery of Iowa City*, with the churches of Iowa City, Providence, Solon, Cedar Rapids, Mount Vernon, Pleasant Prairie, Brush Run, Marengo, Benton, Vinton, Centre Point, Waterloo, Cedar Falls, Janesville, Clarksville, La Fayette, Indian Creek, Newton, and Lyons.

4. *The Presbytery of Dubuque*, recently formed, with the church of Dubuque and other congregations in that part of the State.

This Synod has a Church Erection Fund of about two thousand dollars, independent of the Assembly's fund; also a college at Yellow Spring, in Des Moines County, together with a female seminary at Keokuk, and other Academic institutions for both sexes, at Cedar Rapids, Vinton and Troy.

Mr. L. B. Parsons, late of Wyoming, N. Y., deceased, has, it is reported, bequeathed property, valued at forty or fifty thousand dollars, for a college connected with this branch of the church.

PRESBYTERIAN CHURCH. (O. S.)

The Synod of Iowa is divided into three Presbyteries. Having received no statement for 1855, we insert those of 1854 :—

	No. Members.	No. Churches.
1. Presbytery of Iowa........................	247	24
2. Presbytery of Cedar........................	799	47
3. Presbytery of Des Moines............	787	100
In Synod of Iowa	1833	171

Location of Presbyterian Churches.

First Presbytery.—Keokuk, West Point, Middletown, Morning Sun, Mount Pleasant, Charleston, Burlington, Lowell, Spring Creek, Fort Madison,and Kossuth. *Second Presbytery.*—Muscatine, West Liberty, Farmer's Creek, Tipton, Scotch Grove, Cascade, Grandview, Marion, Lime Grove, Dubuque, Davenport, Iowa City, Le Claire, Solon, Blue Grass, Maquoketa, Postville, Franckville, Colesburg, Lybrand, Pleasant Grove, Vinton, Independence, Hopkinton, Lisbon, Princeton. *Third Presbytery.* — Fairfield, Libertyville, Sigourney, Birmingham, Winchester, Oskaloosa, Washington, Brighton, Albia, Crawfordsville, Troy, Keosauqua, Bentonsport, Kirkville, Indianolo, Ottumwa, Knoxville, and Fort Des Moines.

PROTESTANT EPISCOPAL CHURCH IN THE DIOCESE OF IOWA.

Organized Parishes.

Church of the Advent.............................. Danville.
Christ Church.. Burlington.

Grace Church	Cedar Rapids.
Hope Church	Fort William.
St. James' Church	Oskaloosa.
St. John's Church	Keokuk.
St. John's Church	Dubuque.
St. Paul's Church	Bellevue.
St. Paul's Church	Ft. Des Moines.
Trinity Church	Muscatine.
Trinity Church	Davenport.
Trinity Church	Washington.
Trinity Church	Iowa City.
Trinity Church	Fairfield.
Grace Church	Lyons.
St. John's Church	Clinton.
St. Luke's Church	Lansing.
St. Mark's Church	Fort Dodge.

List of the Clergy.

The Rt. Rev. HENRY W. LEE, D. D., Bishop of the Diocese.

The Rev. WILLIAM ADDERLY, Missionary at Fort Madison, Washington, and Fairfield.

The Rev. JOHN BATCHELDER, Rector of the Church of the Advent, Danville, and Missionary for Des Moines County.

The Rev. R. D. BROOKE, Rector of St. John's Church, Dubuque.

The Rev. GEORGE DENNISON, Rector of St. John's Church, Keokuk.

The Rev. FRANKLIN R. HAFF, Rector of Christ Church, Burlington.

The Rev. JAMES KEELER, residing near Cedar Falls.

The Rev. A. LOUDERBACK, Rector of Trinity Church, Davenport.

The Rev. EDWARD W. PEET, Rector of St. Paul's Church, Fort Des Moines.

The Rev. SAMUEL STARR, Rector of Grace Church, Cedar Rapids.

The Rev. C. C. TOWNSEND, Rector of Trinity Church, Iowa City.

The Rev. JOHN UFFORD, Rector of Trinity Church, Muscatine.

The Rev. GEORGE W. WATSON, Rector of St. Paul's Church, Bellevue.

The Rev. H. W. BEERS, Rector of Grace Church, Lyons.

The Rev. W. H. BARRIS, Rector of Trinity Church, Iowa City.

The Rev. P. A. JOHNSON, Rector of St. James' Church, Oskaloosa.

The Rev. GEORGE C. STREET, Davenport.

The territorial limits of the diocese embrace the entire State. It was organized into a diocese, August 18th, 1853, under the provisionary charge of the Rt. Rev. J. Kemper, D. D. The present bishop was elected June 1st, 1854.

There are organized parishes in the following places:—Dubuque, Bellevue, Davenport, Muscatine, Burlington, Ft. Madison, Keokuk, Ft. Des Moines, Washington, Iowa City, and Cedar Rapids. Churches are built in the following places:—Dubuque, Davenport, Muscatine, Burlington, and Keokuk, and one is in progress at Cedar Rapids.

The number of clergy in the diocese is 11; number of communicants, about 300. Immigration is adding to families and communicants every month. Number of Sunday Schools not ascertained as yet. The second annual convention meets at Burlington, on the 29th of May next.

Methodist Churches.

In the following table we give a full history of the condition of the Methodist Churches in Iowa, as rendered at the Eleventh Annual Conference, held September 27th, 1854:—

M. E. CHURCHES.

DISTRICTS.	Churches.	Parsonag's.	Preachers.	Members.	DISTRICTS	Churches.	Parsonag's.	Preachers.	Members.
Keokuk.........	22	7	49	4171	Iowa City......	14	6	33	1948
Burlington....	23	10	35	2830	Ft. Des Moines	7	9	41	2882
Dubuque.......	8	5	21	1518	Council Bluffs	3	0	13	408
Upper Iowa ...	15	4	21	1332					
Mt. Vernon....	4	4	30	1374	Total.........	80	41	222	15131

M. E. SABBATH SCHOOLS.

DISTRICTS.	Schools.	Scholars.	Volumes in library.	Converted past year.	DISTRICTS.	Schools.	Scholars.	Volumes in library.	Converted past year.
Keokuk........	52	2650	6263	112	Ft. Des Moines	41	1656	4151	34
Burlington....	39	2496	5615	94	Council Bluffs	11	417	850	3
Dubuque.......	28	1363	4657	9	Scattering.....	4	430	100	6
Upper Iowa ...	42	1851	4595	38					
Mt. Vernon....	35	1146	4229	48	Total.........	271	13,254	35,173	398
Iowa City......	39	1215	3715	35					

Catholic Churches and Clergy.

The diocess of Dubuque, comprises the State of Iowa, and is administered by the Rt. Rev. Mathias Loras, D. D. The principal buildings at Dubuque embrace the "Cathedral of St. Raphael," now nearly completed, the "Holy Trinity," (German), and a new and spacious church in the upper part of the city, "under the patronage of St. Patrick." Also the "Mount St. Bernard Theological Seminary," situated four miles from Dubuque, with ten seminaries and three professors; the "Cistercian Monastery of Our Blessed Lady of La Trappe," New Melleray, near Dubuque; "Brothers of Christian Instruction," at New Paradise Grove, four miles from Dubuque, and "St. Joseph's Female Academy," situated eight miles from Dubuque. Beside the above, the Catholics have the "Convent and Academy of the Visitation," at Keokuk, and churches and stations at the follow ing named places :—

Dubuque County, at Dubuque, Cascade, Green Oak, New Vienna, St. Joseph's, Shellsmound, St. Nicholas, and Téte-de-Mort;

Jackson County, at Garry Owen, St. Lawrence, Cascade Belleview, and Sabula;

Jones County, at Castle Grove, and St. Thomas;

Delaware County, at Buffalo Grove;

Clayton County, at Carnovillo, and Guttenberg;

Clinton County, at Lyons, and Camanche;

Scott County, at Davenport, and Le Claire;

Muscatine County, at Muscatine;

Johnson County, at Iowa City, English River, and Old Man's Creek;

Des Moines County, at Burlington, Dodgeville, and Augusta;

Lee County, at West Point, Fort Madison, Keokuk, and Farmington;

Winnesheik County, at Big Springs, and Old Mission; at Ottumwa, Wapello County; Ft. Des Moines, Polk County; Council Bluffs, Pottawattamie County, and New Paradise Grove, near Mount St. Bernard.

Recapitulation.—Churches, 35; stations, 17; clergymen, 29; religious communities, 5; Catholic academies, 4; Catholic population, 20,000.

[We have not been able to procure statistics of the Christian, the Lutheran, and other denominations. If those interested will forward printed or written statements of their condition, &c., we will take pleasure in inserting them in future editions.]

CHAPTER XXVIII.

BENEVOLENT SOCIETIES.

Free and Accepted Masons.

Location.	No. of Members.	Location.	No. of Members.
Burlington	50	Washington	30
Muscatine	63	Farmington	16
Dubuque	44	New London	32
Iowa City	28	Keokuk	23
Wapello	23	Muscatine	37
Marion	49	Iowa City	20
Augusta	18	Sigourney	30
Mount Pleasant	35	Winchester	21
Keosauqua	46	De Witt	23
Tipton	26	Kirkville	24
Keokuk	29	Maquoketa	16
Fort Madison	18	Davenport	28
Bloomfield	33	Richland	11
Fairfield	35	Sabula	20
Ottumwa	25	Troy	16
Salem	49	Libertyville	23
Oskaloosa	47	Centreville	14
Lyons	—	Wintersett	15
Burlington	23	Le Claire	13
Agency City	34	Crawfordville	13
Ft. Des Moines	18	Anamosa	11
Grandview	17	Bentonsport	7
Rochester	17	Cedar Falls	—
Cedar Rapids	28		

NOTE.—This table is taken from the Report made to the Grand Annual Communication, June 6th, 1854. Other lodges have been organized since, and numerous members added to the Order, but this is the latest reliable data accessible. In this list the lodges are arranged according to their age and No., except that one (No. 9), "revoked," is omitted; so that Mount Pleasant is No. 8, Keosauqua, 10, Tipton, 11, &c. The next session of the Grand Lodge of Iowa, will be held in Keosauqua, Van Buren County, the first Tuesday in June, 1856.

Independent Order of Odd Fellows.

There are of the I. O. of O. F. in this State, sixty-one lodges, which are located in the following counties:—

Appanoose,	Fayette,	Mahaska,
Buchanan,	Henry,	Madison,
Black Hawk,	Jackson,	Muscatine,
Bremer,	Jefferson,	Pottawattamie,
Clayton,	Johnson,	Polk,
Cedar,	Jones,	Scott,
Clinton,	Keokuk,	Van Buren,
Delaware,	Lee,	Wappello,
Dubuque,	Louisa,	Washington,
Des Moines,	Lima,	Winnesheik,
Davis,	Marion,	Warren.

Sons of Temperance.

The number of divisions of Sons of Temperance in the State, as near as we can ascertain, is not far from one hundred and fifty, most of which are located as follows:—

Counties.	Towns.
Appanoose,	Centreville.
Black Hawk,	Waterloo.
Cedar,	Rochester, Springdale.
Clinton,	De Witt, Camanche.
Davis,	Bloomfield.
Delaware,	Delhi, Hopkinton, Uniontown.

Counties.	Towns.
Des Moines,........................	Burlington.
Dubuque,........................	Dubuque, Hogansville.
Henry,........................	Mount Pleasant, Salem.
Jackson,........................	Andrew, Bellevue, S. Fork, Sabula, Lamotte.
Jasper,........................	Newton.
Jefferson,........................	Fairfield, Glasgow.
Johnson,........................	Iowa City.
Keokuk,........................	Sigourney.
Lee,........................	Keokuk.
Louisa,........................	Toolsboro'.
Lucas,........................	Chariton.
Mahaska,........................	Hopewell, Oskaloosa.
Marion,........................	Knoxville.
Monroe,........................	Albia.
Mills,........................	Silver Creek, Glenwood.
Polk,........................	Ft. Des Moines.
Scott,........................	Davenport, Le Claire, Blue Grass.
Van Buren,........................	Keosauqua, Farmington, Pittsburg.
Wapello,........................	Ottumwa, Dahlonega, Agency City, Eddyville, Bentonsport, Bonaparte, Birmingham.
Washington,........................	Washington, Richmond.
Warren,........................	Indianola.

CHAPTER XXIX.

PUBLIC IMPROVEMENTS.

OF Public improvements in Iowa, probably the more important and extensive are those now in progress by the Des Moines Navigation and Railroad Company. This company was organized in May, 1854, with a capital of $3,000,000. They hold a grant from Congress, embracing all the alternate sections of public lands, for the distance of five miles on each side of the Des Moines River, consisting of about 1,000,000 acres of the best land in the State; also the right to collect such toll and water-rents as they may deem proper for the term of 75 years. The improvement of the Des Moines River is to be made by the construction of a slack water navigation, from the Mississippi to Fort Des Moines, by means of dams and locks, and occasionally by short canals, parallel with, but independent of the river. The average distance between the dams is about seven miles, and the average lift of the locks is ten feet. This company have entered into bonds with the State that the locks and dams shall be completed so as to ensure the navigation of the Des Moines River from the Mississippi to Fort Des Moines, a distance of about two hundred miles, by the 1st of July 1858. The total expenses already incurred on account of the work is $562,457 21. It is probable that 600,000 acres of the choice lands of this company will be sold during the next four years, at about eight dollars per acre, one-fourth down, balance in ten equal annual payments. This company have also a Railroad line along the Des Moines Valley, which will eventually extend into Minnesota. This road is contracted to be open from Keokuk to Bentonsport early in 1857. Particulars of either branch of this great work may be had by addressing Henry O'Reilly, Esq., Secretary, at Ottumwa, Iowa.

The Mississippi Rapids Improvement, is also an important Public Work. The Rapids occur in the river, and are 12 miles in length, terminating at Keokuk, and 13 miles in length, terminating at Davenport. The fall on the Lower Rapids is 24 feet, on the Upper Rapids about 16 feet; and on either sufficient to check, and at times prevent, navigation during a season of low water. Some six years ago, a company was formed to construct a canal on the Iowa side of the Lower Rapids, 250 feet wide, which would give four feet of water at the lowest stage, and with a fall of 24 feet in 12 miles, would afford an extensive site for mills and manufactories. Colonel Curtis, of Keokuk, an experienced engineer, states that this canal plan is the safest, cheapest, most expeditious, and most practicable plan that can be adopted. He says a substantial embankment, well protected by stone, and all other necessary improvements can be constructed in the Lower Rapids for $1,000,000. Lieutenant Warren estimates the cost of the same improvements at $4,000,000. We predict that the immense water-power at this great commercial city will not always pass idly by—and if practicable, either of the above estimates would prove a judicious expenditure, be it a public or private enterprise. An appropriation of $1,000,000 has been made by Congress for excavating the Channel in these Rapids, and some progress made during the past two years. Major John G. Floyd, Civil Engineer of the Rapids Improvement, states that by an annual appropriation of $200,000, a well defined, safe, and convenient channel, 200 feet wide and 4 feet deep can be secured. It is probable a thorough trial will be made by Major Floyd to remove these obstructions by excavation.

Of Railroads.—As the observer will readily decide, upon reading the following list of Railroads, which are actually being built, there is probably no other State in the Union that will put into operation more miles of Railroad during any one or all of the ten years to come, than Iowa. The routes of each of these Railroads, and also of those projected in the State, will be found correctly drawn upon "*Parker's Sectional and Geological Map of Iowa.*"

Burlington and Missouri—to be completed to Ottumwa on the Des Moines River, in November, 1856.

Chicago, Iowa, and Nebraska—from Clinton *via* Cedar Rapids and Fort Dodge, to Sergeant's Bluff—contracted to be completed, 40 miles, in 1856.

Dubuque and Pacific—projected to Sergeant's Bluff—to be completed to Delhi, 30 miles, 15th November, 1856.

Fort Madison and Bloomfield—to be completed in thirty months.

Iowa Central Air Line—from Lyons, *via* Maquoketa,

through central tier of counties, west—under contract to Maquoketa.

Keokuk, Fort Des Moines, and Minnesota—contracted to be completed to Bentonsport in 1856.

Keokuk, Mount Pleasant, and Muscatine Railroad—the first Division from Keokuk to Montrose to be completed by July, 1856.

Mississippi and Missouri—the Pioneer Road—already completed to Iowa City—under contract to Fort Des Moines.

These Railroads are all needed, and each bid fair to be completed at an early day.

Among the most important Public Works projected in the West, is "The People's Highway," between the Atlantic and Pacific States, with postal and telegraphic facilities, incidental to the protection of settlers and immigrants between the Mississippi Valley and the Pacific Ocean. This important enterprise was first projected and will be perfected by General Henry O'Reilly, who has had great experience in the establishment of Telegraph lines throughout the United States. His memorial to Congress was presented and favorably considered at its last session, and will probably be complied with, the present session. His system of intercommunication has met with the approval and recommendation of the Governors of Missouri, Iowa, and Nebraska; and also of the National Telegraph and Railroad Convention, in which the States of Missouri, Illinois, Indiana, Kentucky, Pennsylvania, New York, Ohio, Iowa, Wisconsin, Michigan, Virginia, Tennesse, New

Jersey and Louisiana, were represented. The present laws provide for a line of military posts from the Mississippi Valley to the Pacific. Mr. O'Reilly asks neither money nor especial favor from the Federal Government, but that instead of establishing a large number of men at each post, the number of stations be increased, so that they may be twenty miles apart and only twenty men at each post; and that two or three soldiers shall ride daily, each way, from each stockade, furnishing the three-fold purpose of transmitting a daily letter mail from station to station, protecting a Telegraph Line from molestation, and affording escort and assistance to immigrants and settlers.

This enterprise is to a great portion of the West, especially the "Far West," second in importance to none other, and having been pronounced by the best of judges as perfectly practicable, we earnestly hope the project may be carried out. General O'Reilly is now a resident of Iowa, and the completion of his great work would give Iowa a through line of Telegraph, east and west, and place her upon the great Atlantic and Pacific Line.

CHAPTER XXX.

LIST OF POST OFFICES IN IOWA, ARRANGED ALPHABETICALLY IN COUNTIES.

[NOTE.—The names of all the counties in the State are here given—those that have no Post-Offices named therein, are not yet organized.]

ADAIR COUNTY.

Adair.
Alconus.
Holaday's.
Marvin's.
Wahtahwah.

ADAMS COUNTY.

Icaria.
Quincy.

ALAMAKEE COUNTY.

Bellows.
Bryson.
Bunker Hill.
Capoli.
Columbus.
French Creek.
Grantville.
Hardin.
Ion.
Lansing.
Lybrand.
Lycurgus.
Markee.
Ossian.
Painted Rock.
Postville.
Rossville.
Union Prairie.
Volney.
Waterville.
Wawkon.
Wexford.

APPANOOSE COUNTY.

Centreville.
Cincinnati.
Hibbsville.
Iconium.
Moravia.
Milliard.
Mt. Gilead.
Pleasant View.
Sharon.
Unionville.
Wells' Mills.

AUDUBON COUNTY.

Ballard.
Bear Grove.
Hamlin Grove.

BENTON COUNTY.

Benton City.
Beulah.
Burke.
Marysville.
Taylor's Grove.
Vinton.

BLACKHAWK COUNTY.

Barclay.
Cedar Falls.
Eliza.
Elk River.

Enterprise.
Knox.
Laporte City.
Sturgess Rapids.
Waterloo.

BOONE COUNTY.

Bellepointe.
Boonsboro.
Mineral Ridge.
Parkersburg.
Rapids.
Ridge.
Sweed Point.

BREMER COUNTY

Jackson Point.
Janesville.
Neutral.
Waverly.

BUCHANAN COUNTY.

Brandon.
Buffalo Grove.
Chatham.
Erin.
Frink's Grove.
Greely's Grove.
Independence.
Pine.
Quasqueton.

BUTLER COUNTY.

Beaver Grove.
Clarksville.
Leoni.

BUENA VISTA COUNTY.

BUNCOME COUNTY.

CALHOUN COUNTY.

CARROLL COUNTY.

CASS COUNTY.

Edna.
Iranistan.
Lewis.
Lura.
Pymosa.

CEDAR COUNTY.

Cedar.
Cambridge.
Gower's Ferry.
Harwell.
Honey Grove.
Inland.
Lacton.
Massillon.
Onion Grove.
Pedee.
Pioneer Grove.
Red Oak.
Rochester.
Rosette.
Springdale.
Tipton.
West Branch.
Woodbridge.

CERRO GORDO COUNTY.

Clear Lake.

CHEROKEE COUNTY.

CLAY COUNTY.

CLARKE COUNTY.

Bartletteville.
Glenns.
Hopeville.
Hickory Grove.
Laporte.
Milford.
Norris.
Osceola.
Ottawa.
White Breast.

CLAYTON COUNTY.

Brookville.
Buena Vista.
Clayton.
Communia.
Council Hill.
Elkader.
Elkport.
Farmersburg.
Garnavillo.
Girard.
Grand Meadow.
Guttenburg.
High Grove.
Highland.
Littleporte.
Lodomills.
McGregor's Landing.
Millville.
Monona.
National.
Newstand.
Panther Creek.
Sylvan.
Strawberry Point.
Sodomville.
Volga City.

CLINTON COUNTY.

Boone Spring. Brookfield. Buena Vista. Burgess. Camanche. Charlotte. Cherry Wood. Clinton. De Witt. Elk River. Elvira. Grand Mound. Lyons. Orange. Spring Rock. Toronto. Welton.

CHICKASAW COUNTY.

Bradford. Chickasaw. New Hampton.

CRAWFORD COUNTY.

DALLAS COUNTY.

Adell. Boone. McKay. Uncle Sam. Wiscotta.

DAVIS COUNTY.

Bloomfield. Chequist. Del Norte. Drakesville. Floris. Monterey. Mt. Calvary. Nottingham. Oak Spring. Pulaski. Roscoe. Salt Creek. Savannah. Soap Creek. Stiles. Stringtown. Taylor. Troy. Weep'g Willow. West Grove.

DECATUR COUNTY.

Decatur. Franklin. Garden Grove. Hungarian Settlement. Leon. New Buda. Nine Eagles. Turkey Run.

DES MOINES COUNTY.

Albright's. Augusta. Burlington. Danville. Dale. Dodgeville. Hawk Eye. Huron. Hartford. Kingston. Kossuth. Limestone. Linton. Middletown. Northfield. Oakland. Parish. Pleasant Grove. South Flint. Yellow Springs.

DELAWARE COUNTY.

Bailey's Ford. Burrington. Coffin's Grove. Cold Water. Colesburg. Coluny. Delhi. Delaware Centre. Dyesville. Forrestville. Green Hill. Grove Creek. Hopkinton. Hartwick. Mount Hope. Oakland. Orrinden. Plum Spring. Poultney. Rockville. Springbranch. Uniontown. Viola.

DICKINSON COUNTY.

DUBUQUE COUNTY.

Alma. Aspinwall. Buncome. Cascade. Centralia. Charmingville. Cottage Hill. Dubuque. Durango. Epworth. Evergreen. Fillmore. Glassnevin. Hogansville. Mileray. New Vienna. Pin Oak. Peru. Tivoli. Viola. Welds' Landing.

EMMETT COUNTY.

FAYETTE COUNTY.

Clermont.
Douglass.
Eden.
Eldorado.
Fayetteville.
Gamble Grove.
Illyria.
Leo.
Linn.
Louisville.
Mill Grove.
Taylorsville.
Waucoma.
Westfield.
Windsor.
West Union.

FLOYD COUNTY.

Freeman.
Floyd Centre.
Gilmantown.

FRANKLIN COUNTY.

FRÉMONT COUNTY.

Austin.
Cory.
Dawsonburgh.
Gaston.
Manti.
McKissack's Grove.
Osage.
Sidney.
Tabor.

GREENE COUNTY.

GRUNDY COUNTY.

GUTHRIE COUNTY.

Allen
Bear Grove.
Panora.
Pennsbury.

HANCOCK COUNTY.

HARRISON COUNTY.

Calhoun.
Fontainbleau.
Magnolia.

HARDIN COUNTY.

Alden.
Eldora.
Hardin.
Poughkeepsie.
Rockwood.

HENRY COUNTY.

East Grove.
Hillsborough.
Lowell.
Marshall.
Mt. Pleasant.
New London.
Rome.
Salem.
Trenton.
Vega.
Wayne.
Winfield.

HOWARD COUNTY.

New Oregon.

IDA COUNTY.

IOWA COUNTY.

Cono.
Dayton.
Downard.
Homestead.
Jones.
Kozta.
Marengo.
Millersburg.
North English.
Prairie Creek.
Williamsburg.

JACKSON COUNTY.

Andrew.
Bellevue.
Bridgeport.
Canton.
Cobb.
Cottonville.
Copper Creek.
Emeline.
Farmer's Creek
Fulton.
Garry Owen.
Hickory Grove.
Higgensport.
Iron Hills.
Lamonte.
Maquoketa.
Monmouth.
Newton.
Ozark.
Rolley.

Sabula.
Solon.
Spring Brook.
Spruce Mills.
Sterling.
Sullivan.
Summer Hill.
Van Buren.
Waterford.
Wickliffe.

JASPER COUNTY.

Con.
Elliott.
Elk Creek.
Lynville.
Monroe.
Morristown.
North Skunk River.
Parkersburg.

JEFFERSON COUNTY.

Abingdon.
Absecom.
Batavia.
Brookville.
Blue Point.
Deedsville.
Fairfield.
Germanville.
Glasgow.
Harmony.
Libertyville.
Lockridge.
Pleasant Plain.
Salina.
Webster.
Walnut Creek.
Wooster.

JOHNSON COUNTY.

Carthage.
Copi.
Frank Pierce.
Hueston.
Iowa City.
Morfordsville.
Newport.
Newp't Centre.
Solon.
Seventy-Eight.
Seventy-Seven.
Windham.

JONES COUNTY.

Anamosa.
Bowen's Pr'rie.
Castle Grove.
Duane.
Fairview.
Grove Creek.
Highl'nd Gr've.
Johnson.
Marshfield.
Massilon.
Madison.
Monticello.
Pierce.
Rome.
Scotch Grove.
Walnut Fork.

KEOKUK COUNTY.

Butler.
Olean.
Richland.
Sigourney.
South English.
Springfield.
Steady Run.
Warner's Mill.
Webster.
Wimer's Mills.

KOSSUTH COUNTY.

Algona.
Cresco.
Johnson's Settlement.

LEE COUNTY.

Ambrosia.
Big Mound.
Camargo.
Charleston.
Denmark.
Dover.
Fort Madison.
Fr'nklin C'ntre.
Green Bay.
Keokuk.
Montrose.
New Boston.
Pilot Grove.
Primrose.
String Prairie.
Summittville.
West Point.

LINN COUNTY.

Boulder.
Cedar Rapids.
Central Point.
Forfax.
Hoosier Grove.
Ivanhoe.
Lafayette.
Lisbon.
Marion.
Mon Dieu.
Mount Vernon.
Necot.
Oak Grove.
Palo.
Prospect Hill.
St. Julien.
St. Mary's.
Spring Grove.
Springville.
Valley Farm.

LOUISA COUNTY.

Concord.
Columbus City.
Grand View.
Harrison.
Hope Farm.
Morning Sun.
Palo Alto.
Port Allen.
Port Louisa.
Spring Glenn.
Toolsborough.
Virginia Grove.
Wapello.

LUCAS COUNTY.

Argo.
Cedar Grove.
Chariton.
Freeland.
Greenville.
La Grange.
Tallahoma.

MADISON COUNTY.

Bibb's Ridge.
North Branch.
Peru.
St. Charles.
Winterset.

MARSHALL COUNTY.

Albion.
Le Grand.
Lafayette.
Marietta.
Marshaltown.
Mormon Hill.
Timber Creek.

MARION COUNTY.

Attica.
Bennington.
Columbia.
Ely.
English Settlement.
Gosport.
Hamilton.
Iola.
Knoxville.
Marysville.
Newbern.
Pella.
Pleasantville.
R. Cedar Mills.
Red Rock.
Wheeling.

MILLS COUNTY.

Cerro Gordo.
Florence.
Glenwood.
Indian Creek.
Ingraham.
Wahoghbonsy.

MAHASKA COUNTY.

Agricola.
Auburn.
Bellefontaine.
Blue Creek.
Fremont.
Granville.
Hopewell.
Indianapolis.
Nine Mile.
Oskaloosa.
Peoria.
Rose Hill.
Scott.

MONROE COUNTY.

Avery.
Albia.
Cuba.
Gray's Creek.
H'fway Prairie.
Sovilia.
Lucas.
Mantua.

MITCHELL COUNTY.

Cora.
Mitchell.
Osage.

MONONA COUNTY.

Ashton.
Preparation.

MONTGOMERY COUNTY.

Frankford.
Sciola.

MUSCATINE COUNTY.

Centre Grove.
Fairport.
Melpine.
Moscow.
Muscatine.
Pike.
Strawb'ry Hill.
Sweetland Centre.
West Liberty.

O'BRIEN COUNTY.

OSCEOLA COUNTY.

PAGE COUNTY.

Centre. Nodaway.
Clarinda. Tarkio.
Hawleyville.

PALO ALTO COUNTY.

PLYMOUTH COUNTY.

POCAHONTAS COUNTY.

POLK COUNTY.

Apple Grove. Hopkins Grove.
Circleville. Midway.
Eckhart. Polk City.
Ft. Des Moines. Rising Sun.
Freel. Saylorville.
Hartman. Summerset.

POTTAWATTAMIE COUNTY.

Americus. Macedonia.
Big Grove. Prairie Flower.
Council Bluffs. Silver Creek.

POWESHEIK COUNTY.

Bear Creek. Montezuma.
Deep River. Sugar Grove.
Grinnell. Victor.

RINGGOLD COUNTY.

Mount Air.

SAC COUNTY.

New Munich.

SCOTT COUNTY.

Allen's Grove. Big Rock.
Amity. Blue Grass.
Davenport. Pleasant Valley
Fulton. Princeton.
Le Claire. Walnut Grove.
LeClaire Centre West Buffalo.
Linn Grove. Wolcott.

SHELBY COUNTY.

Shelbyville.

SIOUX COUNTY.

STORY COUNTY.

Goshen. Nevada.

TAMA COUNTY.

Indiantown. Red Man.
Kinisaw. Tamaville.
Ola. Toledo.

TAYLOR COUNTY.

Grove. Gravity.

UNION COUNTY.

Afton. Kings.

VAN BUREN COUNTY.

Bentonsport. Mt. Sterling.
Birmingham. New Market.
Bonaparte. Oak Point.
Business C'rn'r Pameka.
Farmington. Philadelphia.
Gainesborough. Pittsburgh.
Home. Portland.
Iowaville. Union.
Keosauque. Upton.
Lebanon. Utica.
Lick Creek. Vernon.
Milton. Winchester.

WARREN COUNTY.

Carlisle. Lynn.
Dorriville. Montpelier.
Fort Plain. Palmyra.
Greenhurst. Plainville.
Hammondsb'g. Sandyville.
H'ndsome View Wilmington.
Hartford. White Oak.
Indianola.

WASHINGTON COUNTY.

Amboy. Pottsville.
Brighton. Richmond.
Clay. Valley.
Crawfordsville. Washington.
Davis Creek. Wassonville.
Dutch Creek. Yatton.
Marcellus.

WAYNE COUNTY.

Bethlehem. Grand River.
Cambria. South Fork.
Corydon. Warsaw.
Freedom.

WAPELLO COUNTY.

Agency City. Chillicothe.
Ashland. Competine.
Blakesburg. Cotton Grove.
Dahlonega. Kirkville.
Dorrville. Ottumwa.
Eddyville. Pleasant Lake.
Fountain Sp'g. Point Isabelle.
Greene.

WEBSTER COUNTY.

Border Plains. Dakotah.
Cresco, (no P.O. yet.) Homer.
Fort Dodge. Webster City.

WINNESHEIK COUNTY.

Burr Oak. Freeport.
Calmar. Moneek.
Castalia. Old Mission.
Decorah. Ossian.
Ft. Atkinson. Trout River.
Frankville. Winnesheik.

WINNEBAGO COUNTY.

WOODBURY COUNTY.

Floyd's Bluff. Serg'nt's Bluff City.
Sioux City.

WORTH COUNTY.

WRIGHT COUNTY.

THE END.

www.ingramcontent.com/pod-product-compliance
Lightning Source LLC
LaVergne TN
LVHW020242110826
845151LV00003B/1007

9781425529048